Mining the Motherlode

Was this her dissertation?

Mining the Motherlode

METHODS IN WOMANIST ETHICS

Stacey M. Floyd-Thomas

THE
PILGRIM
PRESS
Cleveland

Dedicated to
Mary Elizabeth Underwood,
Lillian Underwood Floyd,
and Janet Floyd —
the three women who by nature and nurture
cultivated my womanish spirit.

The Pilgrim Press
700 Prospect Avenue
Cleveland, Ohio 44115-1100
thepilgrimpress.com

Printed in the United States of America on acid-free paper

10 09 08 07 06   5 4 3 2 1

Library of Congress Cataloging-in-Publication Data

Floyd-Thomas, Stacey M., 1969-
  Mining the motherlode : methods in womanist ethics / Stacey M.
  Floyd-Thomas.
      p. cm.
  Includes bibliographical references and index.
  ISBN 0-8298-1584-8
  1. Christian ethics. 2. Womanist theology. I. Title.
BJ1278.F45F56 2006
241.082 — dc22
                                                          2005028970
ISBN-13 978-0-8298-1584-9
ISBN-10 0-8298-1584-8

Contents

Foreword

Can only African American women be womanists? Precisely, what attributes are included when we assert that a particular person is a womanist? Is it an insensitive abuse of privilege when colleagues insist that anyone who so desires can be an avowed, practicing womanist regardless of race, creed, or color? *Mining the Motherlode: Methods in Womanist Ethics* is an important text that gathers together examples of theological and pedagogical answers to this ontological inquiry and helps us focus on the ongoing tasks of liberation. This offering by Stacey Floyd-Thomas is a bonanza, a treasure trove of succinctly delineated methodologies for justice-seekers called to action, away from nihilistic complacency, reminding us of the mediating role between theory and praxis.

Ever since my first conversation with Stacey Floyd-Thomas, during her matriculation as my doctoral student in the Department of Religion at Temple University, she readily expressed a vocational vision of unraveling the complex web of normative ethics and speaking out against massive evil inherent in a white supremacist patriarchal social order. At that point in our dialogue, I shared with her my illustration of what mining the motherlode means for black intellectuals. The fundamental characteristic of a worthwhile scholarly life is the search for sustaining nourishment for our souls.

Several summers ago, while teaching in Los Angeles, I stayed on the tree-lined campus of Mount Saint Mary's College. One of the things that fascinated me the most as I walked between buildings and grounds was how the roots of huge magnolia trees spread out every which way. Tree roots ran in all kinds of directions. Some of the roots of these magnolia trees were exposed at least two and three feet above ground — seeking, always searching, for life-giving nourishment. This thick network of tree roots encircled many other plants, but this did not matter to the magnolia trees because the magnolia trees were hunting for the fount, the mainspring, the motherlode of life.

I am enormously impressed in the way Dr. Floyd-Thomas mines the motherlode in this text by using scholarly resources, demonstrating her commitment to interdisciplinary studies, and applying ethical analysis to her research on womanist methodologies, in ways that the subject matter has not hitherto been approached. In addition, she is able to distill from primary texts in Christian ethics the very core of significance and then, in the development of definitive, intellectual arguments, dig down to fundamentals and come up with imaginative and engaging analyses. She skillfully knows how to teach others how to pursue such endeavors. In this regard, Dr. Floyd-Thomas displays a rare combination of scholarship and pedagogy.

Therefore, it is not surprising that Dr. Floyd-Thomas has written this book. In it, she courageously re-imagines theoethics and its cognate disciplines in radical ways. *Mining the Motherlode: Methods in Womanist Ethics* is a text that instills respect for the contributions of both theoretical and practical methodologies. In turn, African American women, and all who cast their lot with us, can train effective and informed ministers and educators about womanist ways of being, thinking, and doing.

Katie G. Cannon

Preface

At an early age I developed an interest in the complex relationship between norms and actions. Although I had neither the scholarly language of ethics nor the axiological framework of sociology of religion necessary to structure my observations, I was nonetheless intrigued to find that the relationship between the theological, quasi-spiritual preaching of many ministers and church leaders — those who arguably had been "called" by God — and the actual practices of these selfsame purveyors of the word of God were not in perfect accord. As I grew older and more aware, it amazed me to discover that, despite what I had been taught in word and song, judging by the actions of my elders, Jesus did not in fact love all the little children of the world. Herein lay the fallacy of my childish moral reasoning: I had assumed that preaching would dictate practice and that thoughts dictate action. That theoethical wrestling marked the beginning of my consideration of the ethicist's supreme query, "Why do people do what they do?"

I realized that what I saw as a child in Corpus Christi (literally translated from Latin as "the body of Christ"), Texas, differed fundamentally from the precepts with which I had been inculcated. What I saw was racial distrust. I saw the perpetuation of sexist stereotypes. I saw the oppression of disadvantaged people by the dominant privileged class. At an early age, I also saw people of one so-called minority group turn against other oppressed people, disavowing any commonalities, any shared history, yet claiming the same spiritual strivings. As a youth, I also remember being disappointed by my local congregation's refusal to include persons who did not fit the community's norms of being religious, while at the same time fully professing Christianity, which I understood to be an inclusive gospel. I witnessed the rejection of the unwed mothers, the unchurched sinner, and the uneducated fool — all rejected because they could not be assimilated comfortably into my middle-class black Baptist environment by the normative standards of that institution. Perhaps the single most damning thing I saw was the tragedy of internalized oppression within a culture by those who did not embody the archetype, or the "norm." To see situations within the black community of my youth in which equally disadvantaged people oppressed and persecuted one another rather than looking out for one another was bad enough. But to realize that such malevolence was often done in the absence of white antagonists was even more distressing. Thus, from early on, I was plagued by these contradictions. My childhood question of "How could so-called Christians behave as if God never existed?" only escalated during my intellectual and theological formation as a graduate student: *Is there a qualitative nature to oppression? How can those who have been most oppressed subscribe to a theology of oppression? Where is the love of God in the sufferings facing "the least of these"? And how ought I, a black woman, live in this world while being counted both the ranks of among the oppressed and the oppressor?*

This ethical contradiction, illuminated by sacred texts and social practices, was a warning sign to me about the being-thinking-doing trichotomy, in which the marginalized wrestle with notions of theodicy while being imprisoned by colonizing forces of sacred rhetoric. Unlike Isis, the goddess of Africa, or the regal "black and beautiful" beloved denoted in the biblical Song of Songs, black American women's real-life experiences in recent centuries illustrate the double jeopardy of being born black and female.

The stereotypical images of the effacing mammy, matriarch, welfare queen, bitch, villain, Sapphire, jezebel, and "gangsta ho'" are projected daily onto black American women, thereby rendering them

begrimed and flawed. Cast in this depraved state, black women experience an ongoing cognitive dissonance in their lifelong journey for
self-realization and social empowerment. That empowerment must
come from some source either within themselves or beyond human
control, for it certainly does not come from society at large. A salient
example of this cognitive dissonance can be found in Alice Walker's
novel *The Color Purple*. Here the novel's central character, Celie —
the once-confused and God-fearing Christian who was taught to worship a god who was a big, tall, white, old, bearded, banker-looking
barefooted man with cool bluish-gray eyes — finds herself wanting
more and ends up disavowing a god to whom she once bared her soul.
In a letter to her sister, Nettie, she writes:

> I don't write to God no more, I write you.
> What happen to God? ast Shug.
> Who that? I say.
> She look at me serious.
> Big a devil as you is, I say, you not worried bout no God,
> surely.
> She say, Wait a minute. Hold on just a minute here. Just
> because I don't harass it like some peoples us know don't mean
> I ain't got religion.
> What God do for me? I ast.
> She say, Celie! Like she shock. He gave you life, good health,
> and a good woman that love you to death.
> Yeah, I say, and he gave me a lynched daddy, a crazy mama,
> a lowdown dog of a step pa and a sister I probably won't ever
> see again. Anyhow, I say, the God I been praying and writing to
> is a man. And act just like all the other mens I know. Trifling,
> forgitful and lowdown.
> She say, Miss Celie, You better hush. God might hear you.
> Let 'im hear me, I say. If he ever listened to poor colored
> women the world would be a different place....[1]

Like Celie, contemporary black women continue to wrestle with reconciling the miserable returns that have met their social investment with the professing of an abundant faith and moral urgency. Yet, even as they persist, they still insist that the world would be a better place if others could see it from their perspective. Here, in this place of existential angst and eschatological hope, black women's insistence on "making a way out of no way," "lifting as they climb," "hitting a straight lick with a crooked stick," and "pressing on the upward way" represents the moral wisdom and spiritual fortitude of those who have been silenced and made invisible in the task of normative theological ethics. These women, despite marked advances in the social and political order of American society, are still deemed little more than three-fifths human. As a result, they are never afforded the status of being a *responsible self* in the normative ethical gaze of H. Richard Niebuhr. Recall that Niebuhr presumes the responsible self to be a moral agent who has the power and autonomy to exercise freedom in relating to God and neighbor. Such agency is unavailable within the everyday reality of the black woman because she has neither the power nor social regard with which she can engage "man" or God. Her experience of what it means to be human is thus denied. Furthermore, the black woman's experience of what it means to be an embodied human exposes John Rawls's classic theory of justice as an absurdity because it disregards envisioning a justice for human beings who are actually embodied people. This moral reflective weakness is not exclusive to scholars alone; even everyday black women are mystified by ordinary well-intentioned and God-fearing people who claim to see the humanity in everyone, yet are frequently ignorant of issues of gender, class, and race at work in their midst.

What do we do with these disinherited of our world, nation, state, cities, communities, schools, and homes? How can we de-center ourselves from our privileged positions of comfort while simultaneously placing at the center of our thoughts and actions the constructive envisioning offered to us by the most marginalized amongst us? This is my paramount concern as a scholar-activist, and this is what I hope is an urgent question for the church today. But the heart of the problem is not making God a raced, sexed, embodied entity, but rather seeing in every being's race, gender, sex, and class a voice and presence of God that needs to be heard and seen. The moral crisis of identity within both the church and society, occasioned by the unending violence, discrimination, poverty, hatred, and terror, is the fear that we may worship a strange god who is blind to gender, class, and color and neither shares nor sees our interests, concerns, and thoughts.

It is the task of Christian social womanist ethics to divest these spiritually bankrupt theological projects by decolonizing the spirit of Christian moral agency. Central to the womanist ethical agenda is to find the moral means by which we, as scholars of religion, theological educators, clergy, and laypeople can overcome the various forms of alienation (social, cultural, physical, geographical, etc.) that have invariably kept black women from realizing a positive sense of religious awareness within themselves as well as in the company of others. Put another way, we need to develop theories and methods that seek to redeem and restore the field of normative theological ethics in a practical way. We thus make it possible for the teaching of theological education and preaching of an unadulterated liberating gospel to race forward and engender a justice that is responsible, relevant, and embodied in the ultimate concerns for us all. My goal in developing interdisciplinary methods for depicting and resolving crises is ethical formation. In particular, my work seeks to mine those untapped motherlodes of moral wisdom spoken by black women, and seen in their minds, hearts, and souls. This is wisdom gleaned from women whose lives give a worm's-eye view of our particular world. Ironically, although often disparaged and undervalued, black women's perspectives represent a model of epistemological privilege that can help us describe, analyze, and empower all oppressed people in order to change our dismal plights into more positive prospects.

Acknowledgments

One does not make or remake anything alone; one cannot ignore the relations one has. To know one's self and one's situation is to know one's company.*

In this book, I reveal what is sacred to me and what serves as the true source of my ethical reflections: the solidarity of others in the work of justice. Throughout the course of this project, I have been fortunate to have a community of solidarity who thought that a book about the methodological musings of womanist ethics and praxeological constructs of black women was needed and could be done. Consequently, this text is a communal text. It belongs to the collective genius of womanist thinking present now in the academy for over two decades, as well as to my family, friends, colleagues, and students who have journeyed with me. Although I cannot possibly mention all those who have offered help and support during the creation of this work, I would like to mention a few.

I express ultimate appreciation first to God and then to my family — my mother and sister, Lillian Floyd and Janet Floyd, as well as to those members of my immediate family who made their transition during the course of my womanist journey thus far — my

---

*Toinette M. Eugene, "On 'Difference' and the Dream of Pluralist Feminism in 'Appropriation and Reciprocity in Womanist/Mujerista/Feminist Work,'" *Journal of Feminist Studies in Religion* 8 (1992): 91.

maternal grandparents, Sidney and Mary Elizabeth Underwood, my father Charles Floyd, and my brothers Jerome and Greg Floyd. I extend appreciation to the members of the Underwood, Floyd, Sinclair, and Thomas clans — all of whom have prayed and celebrated every effort along the way.

I extend special thanks to many of my colleagues, co-laborers, and friends — especially Duane Belgrave, Duana Butler, Carol Duncan, Robert Franklin, Maisha Handy, Rebecca Dixon Kennedy, Terry Kershaw, Cheryl Kirk-Duggan, Cheryl Diggs Lowe, Larry Mamiya, Anthony Pinn, Stephen Ray, and Lynne Westfield. In more than one way, I have benefited from the assistance and critical concern of these special people, which have shaped and refined me in the process of my life work.

My heartfelt gratitude to my students, especially my student assistants, Jerrolyn Eulinberg, Sarah Harris, Deborah Reagan, Jacob Robinson, Justin Wiencowski, and Alphonetta Wines, whose passion for learning about womanist ethics and whose tireless assistance in this process were my ultimate source of inspiration.

I am very grateful for the Wabash Center for Teaching and Learning of Theology and Religion and Brite Divinity School for acknowledging the value of this work by funding the research that went into it.

Warm regards to my Greater St. Stephen First Church family and dear pastor-mentor-friend Dr. Michael A. Bell, and my Brite colleagues, especially Leo Perdue, Mark Toulouse, W. David Nelson, and David Balch, my spirit-helpers who kept me from getting weary on the journey. Special thanks go to Sandy Brandon and Lauren Bryant for their special assistance. And of course, I would like to thank my editor, Ulrike Guthrie, who has been a midwife in the birthing of this work.

Finally, I need to express a lifetime of indebtedness to three sojourners who gave unrelentingly and lovingly to me and this work: my mentor Katie Geneva Cannon, who taught me how to "read and write even when the lights are out"; my collaborator and dear friend Laura Gillman, who has given me hope that white women and black women can be different but not alienated; and my husband, soulmate, and best friend, Juan Floyd-Thomas, who daily shows me how to love with mind, body, and soul ... *Regardless.*

Introduction

Mining the Motherlode

You know where the minefields are . . . there is wisdom. . . . You are in touch with the ancestors . . . and it is from the gut, not rationally figured out. Black women have to use this all the time, of course, the creativity is still there, but we are not fools. . . . We call it the "epistemological privileges of the oppressed." How do you tap that wisdom — name it, mine it, pass it on to the next generation?[1]

— Katie G. Cannon

Mining the Motherlode is my attempt to rationally name and celebrate the tenets, resources, and methods of a womanist Christian social ethics. I do this by showing how racial and gender ideologies as well as social position inform research methods in theological ethics. This text particularly and unapologetically profiles methods of womanist ethics. It helps anyone interested in the methods used by womanist scholars of religion to mine that wealth of wisdom and apply it to the task of divine and social justice for black women and their communities. All these methods — literary analysis, social analysis, or historiography, along with pedagogical strategies for each — are informed by womanist ethicists and are for the purpose of black female empowerment. Yet the goal of this work is not a prescriptive nor normative ethic for the study of black women, nor to establish one norm

1

for how black women should do scholarship. Rather, I am pursuing constructive ethical methods that:

a. articulate the methodological contributions that womanist ethicists have made to the field of Christian ethics in particular and the larger academic arena of interdisciplinary studies in general;

b. distinguish the works of womanist ethicists from *traditional Christian ethics* that takes for granted moral freedom and self-directing agency, while building upon other forms of *liberation ethics* that evaluate life under oppression in order to empower self-directing agency; and

c. uphold black women's moral struggles at the intersections of race, class, and gender as an essential context to inform ethical inquiry and new possibilities for social justice.

Womanist ethics makes a major contribution to the field of Christian ethics by encouraging us to openly examine issues such as racism, sexism, and classism as social evils in need of ethical analysis and ultimately eradication. Although this work aspires to contribute to the field of Christian ethics, much of its content will depart from its mainstream orientations, since the theoretical prescriptions and methods are drawn from people on the margins of traditional Christian ethics. Black women's experiences and moral dilemmas and their perspectives on spiritual and moral development have rarely been used to interpret what informs ethical values in the academy. As a core theological discipline, Christian ethics focus on questions of human agency (free will, moral conscience, and personal character among other things), human relationships (in public and private settings), and human actions (measured as good or evil, just or unjust, responsible, accountable, and the like).[2] Womanist ethics critiques the canonical, theological, and philosophical assumptions of agency existing free from oppression. The ethical tradition has been to see only "white" or "male" agency when observing the human condition while failing to see how race, class, and gender affect people's ability to be self-directing and critically engaged moral agents. Womanist ethics is at the cutting edge of Christian ethics, providing a unified framework by which we can critically analyze moral agents, actions, and relationships of social oppression.

This text makes available to a broad scholarly audience the research orientations that frame womanist ethics. While the methods that I outline draw from traditional disciplinary approaches, they also transform them in order to understand those very people whom normative disciplinary approaches render invisible. In an increasingly diverse and polarized society, such an examination I hope provides corrective tools for scholarly inquiry on issues of human agency, relationships, and actions of marginalized people, and here particularly, of course, of black women.

To date, much of the work in womanist theology and ethics has been based on the confessional critique of black women scholars in religion: Katie G. Cannon's *Black Womanist Ethics*, Jacquelyn Grant's *White Women's Christ, Black Women's Jesus*, Emilie Townes's *Womanist Justice, Womanist Hope*, Delores Williams's *Sister in the Wilderness*, and Marcia Riggs's *Awake, Arise, and Act*. These works are *confessional* because in them black women claim their blackness and femaleness. By naming themselves "womanist," they refuse the assumption of Christian ethics that one must transcend one's social location in order to speak to the universal condition of their humanity. These first-generation womanist works are *groundbreaking* because they challenge the normalizing ethical discourses that have disallowed a fully human-ized portrayal of black women. Womanist ethicists have taken seriously black women both as scholars of religion and subjects worthy of study. Since its emergence over the past twenty years, womanist ethics has been regarded as a legitimate field of study — with one caveat.

While I resonate with the theoretical and confessional perspectives of first-generation womanist scholars, as one from the second I am convinced of the need to avoid the field being marginalized as viable for exploration only by black women. In light of the ground-breaking work done by first-generation womanists, it is now important to unearth these epistemological treasures so that students and scholars of all backgrounds can *do* womanism even if they cannot *be* womanists. Toward this end, this book is a guide for students, educators, and scholars who want to understand the moral wisdom that may be gleaned from those who live in the interstices of tripartite oppression.

In establishing a discourse in second-generation womanist ethics, *Mining the Motherlode* emerges with the same commitment and following the same trajectory as that of first-generation womanist ethics, but it wrestles with the "how" issue of womanist methodologies rather than the "what" and "why" of womanist theoretical orientation. This, then, is an initial effort to illumine not only the varieties of womanist theories and methods but also to shed light on how to apply them in practical, meaningful ways. Thus, as a second-generation womanist work, *Mining the Motherlode* seeks to make the pioneering genius of womanism more accessible by excavating the methodological core of womanist ethics.

Revisiting the Definition of Womanist

In order to understand how the various strains of womanist theories and methodologies have taken shape in womanism's formative years, it is helpful to return to its genesis. With novelist Alice Walker's coining of the term "womanist," one woman's reflection became a liberation movement for many. It is not fortuitous that womanist ethics' genealogy can be traced to the literary canon of Alice Walker. An award-winning novelist and poet laureate, Walker understood that her mission as a black woman writer was to carve out the distinct phases in which her female characters would develop and pass on not just survival skills but also those qualities that embodied the most salient values of black people in general and black women in particular. As a writer, Walker was intent on capturing these cultural values in such a way as to claim as well as give value to the moral wisdom possessed and practiced by black women. As Walker originally envisioned the concept, the four-part definition is as follows:

WOMANIST 1. From *womanish.* (Opp. of "girlish," i.e., frivolous, irresponsible, not serious.) A black feminist or feminist of color. From the black folk expression of mothers to female children, "you acting womanish," i.e., like a woman. Usually referring to outrageous, audacious, courageous or *willful* behavior. Wanting to know more and in greater depth than is considered "good" for one. Interested in grown up doings. Acting grown up. Being grown up. Interchangeable with another black folk expression: "You trying to be grown." Responsible. In charge. *Serious.*

2. *Also:* A woman who loves other women, sexually and/or nonsexually. Appreciates and prefers women's culture, women's emotional flexibility (values tears as natural counterbalance of laughter) and women's strength. Sometimes loves individual men, sexually and/or nonsexually. Committed to survival and wholeness of entire people, male *and* female. Not a separatist, except periodically, for health. Traditionally universalist, as in: "Mama, why are we brown, pink, and yellow, and our cousins are white, beige, and black?" Ans.: "Well, you know the colored race is just like a flower garden, with every color flower represented." Traditionally capable, as in: "Mama, I'm walking to Canada and I'm taking you and a bunch of other slaves with me." Reply: "It wouldn't be the first time."

3. Loves music. Loves dance. Loves the moon. *Loves* the Spirit. Loves love and food and roundness. Loves struggle. Loves the Folk. Loves herself. *Regardless.*

4. Womanist is to feminist as purple is to lavender.[3]

It was with her creation of this term that Walker could effectively name her epistemology and self-identity as a womanist in order to convey the particulars of black women's experience.

The four parts of the definition that Walker used to describe herself in addition to what she gained from the legacy of black women's literary tradition subsequently became the foundational tenets of a movement among black women religious ethicists who immediately perceived womanism as relevant and imperative to their own work. Womanist ethicists have generally distilled ethical principles from this original definition, which I have identified as the four essential tenets of womanist ethics: radical subjectivity, traditional communalism, self-love, and critical engagement.

With Katie G. Cannon's 1985 introduction of the concept of womanism into the lexicon of Christian social ethics, many African American women in the theological disciplines gravitated to Walker's term, seeing it both as a challenge to normative ethical projects and as a confessional statement for their own social justice work.[4]

Since that time, according to Emilie Townes's definition of womanist ethics, it has made "an important distinction between the ethics of the dominant and the ethics of the dispossessed."[5] Traditionally, freedom of choice as a key dimension of moral agency is taken for granted within normative ethics. The mainstream notion of ethics in our society asserts several virtues that presumably lead one to the type of success typical of "rags-to-riches" stories: rugged individualism, thrift, discipline, and hard work. All of this takes for granted that the person in question is operating with a moral sensibility that she embraced freely of her own accord with full understanding of consequences and repercussions. The vanguard of womanist ethicists, which includes the likes of Katie G. Cannon, Emilie Townes, Marcia Riggs, Barbara Holmes, Rosetta Ross, and Joan Martin, view this understanding of moral agency as antithetical to the realities of the oppressed, especially those who experience tripartite oppression at the hands of

crippling capitalism, gender inequality, and racial discrimination. Ostensibly, freedom of this sort is not an option for innumerable men
and women of color, white women, the poor, and underrepresented
people in the United States. As much as we use, abuse, and mis-
use the notion of freedom, the marginalized and oppressed members
of our society confront an endless barrage of social ills in the hopes
of culling out a different sort of freedom that is outside the norm.
In light of such realities, womanist ethics must operate from a social position where choice, personal independence, self-reliance, strict
economy, and voluntary sacrifice are automatically recognized and
rewarded. Consequently, womanist ethics intentionally focuses upon
duties, obligations, and the formation of ethical values through the
eyes of "the least of these." /how does this differ from Harrison's feminist ethic?

Womanism thus provides a fertile ground for religious reflection
and practical application as a thoroughgoing analysis that attends to
whatever is culturally centered, critically analytical, and socially empowering. Such an analysis is not only descriptive but constructive
as well. Whereas Walker's womanism is descriptive in its articulation
of the subjective, communal, self-loving, and critical aspects of black
women's culture and the cult of black womanhood, womanist ethics is
constructive in that it seeks to determine how to eradicate oppressive
social structures that limit and circumscribe the agency of African
American women. Womanist ethical reflection provides descriptive
foundations that lead to analytical constructs for the eradication of
oppression in the lives of black people and, by extension, the rest of
humanity and creation.

But more than just denoting the journey of one black woman literary genius or a scholarly trend and fad, womanism became an answer
for many black women scholars of religion who needed a perspective by which they could constructively envision and reconcile what
has appeared to be an irreconcilable chasm between the theory and
praxis found within much of the existing scholarship in religion, while

"eliminating as far as possible, contradictory directives for character and behavior."[6]

Womanist ethics serves as a clarion call for a new heuristic and academic enterprise that is focused on shifting the margins to the center, placing the most marginalized experiences of black women at the heart of a burgeoning narrative of religious awareness and spiritual empowerment. Womanist ethics affords the academy a moral opportunity of redemption and reciprocity to consider how the Divine becomes manifested in the everyday experience of women like Celie, women who are quite often left out of its discourses. Toward this end, this text, I hope, provides a key to cultivating a liberative ethic for everyone who professes to be on the side of justice as we collaboratively engage in teaching and learning about what I have defined as the four tenets of womanist ethics: radical subjectivity, traditional communalism, redemptive self-love, and critical engagement.

Radical Subjectivity

As illustrated and described in the first part of Walker's definition, a first merit of womanist ethics is its ability to grasp the radically subjective dimension of the "nature vs. nurture" dialectic inherent within black women's moral formation. Here we see a recurring intergenerational interaction (i.e., mother/daughter, woman/child, older woman to younger woman, worldly woman to a naïve woman, etc.), in which a black woman-child's rite of passage, experienced within the dynamic encounter with a more mature black woman, facilitates a process of mentoring and maturation. Detected and guided by mother-wit as precious yet precarious, this process entails learning the moral lessons that will allow her not only to survive but also to subvert the triple jeopardy of racism, sexism, and classism. Like this girl child, a womanist is radical because she claims her agency and has a subjective view of the world in which she is not a victim of circumstance, but rather is a responsible, serious, and in-charge woman. Thus, the intergenerational lesson of radical subjectivity is to wrest one's sense of identity out of the hold of hegemonic normativity, as womanist ethicists show in their work can be done.

Traditional Communalism

Traditional communalism is the second merit of womanist ethics that is informed by the second part of Walker's definition of womanism. Womanist ethicists engage in scholarly compositions that hold them accountable not to their individual whims or personalized localized consciousnesses but rather to the collective values of black history and culture. In illustrating a spirit of traditional communalism, the work of womanist ethicists encompasses not only the personal story of individual women; it also takes into account the various gifts, identities, and concerns of black people in general in order to use every resource available to strengthen the community as a whole. That is to say, while black female scholars in ethics privilege a womanish culture in their texts, they use their writing to illustrate all of the myriad dimensions of black folk life. In doing so they render a better understanding of how black people collectively undo the historically constructed racist-sexist-classist-heterosexist ideologies that have homogenized them in ways that discount the variations of their humanity and that have deprived them of seeing themselves culturally as traditionally capable as well as traditionally universalist, even within the most oppressive of circumstances.

Redemptive Self-Love

Significant in this regard is how *redemptive self-love,* the third tenet in womanist ethics, reemerges as a continuing theme within womanist ethicists' writings. By demystifying the perceptions of black women's bodies, ways, and loves as vile, the intentionality with which black

women writers reconcile black women back to their truer selves is
invaluable in the formation of womanist ethics. As womanist Cheryl
Townsend Gilkes states when looking at this theme in Walker's work:

> If we are to explore the work of Alice Walker for ethical content
> or for direction in constructing ethics and in thinking theologi-
> cally, I think that the most fruitful course is her artful advocacy
> of unconditional love that starts with our acceptance of ourselves
> as divinely and humanly lovable. . . . In my reading of Walker, this
> would make an excellent ethical study encompassing all of her
> work; this love is the greatest issue in human existence and the
> critical point of convergence between her creative thinking and
> the task of Christian ethics.[7]

The death-dealing effects of such dehumanizing stereotypes have
frequently been noted as an underlying theme and critique in womanist theology and ethics.[8] For her part womanist theologian Michele
Jacques notes that Walker's "call to love herself 'regardless' is one
of the most foundationally holistic and revolutionary political actions
African-American women can take," a call that is the hallmark of the
womanist tradition.[9]

Critical Engagement

The fourth tenet of womanist ethics obliges black women to *critically engage their world at the intersection of their oppressions* since they
have borne the brunt of social injustice throughout the history of the
modern world. As a result, they have an unshakable belief that their
survival strategies must entail more than what others have provided
as an alternative. Most obviously as a counterbalance to feminism,
womanism is always cognizant that the life chances and potential of
black women are circumscribed by more than sexism alone. Thus,
the very essence of womanism stands as an indictment and corrective of those movements with which they would presumably share

common ground. Consequently, womanist ethicists particularly assert that it is womanism in its interlocking analysis of oppression — not white feminism, black liberation, nor Marxist thought with their one-dimensional analyses — that holds the standard and normative measure for true liberation. Womanist ethics mandates that for black women, true liberation necessitates no compromise, mortgage, or trade-off. What it means to be a black woman in this regard is to struggle ceaselessly to the fullest extent in search of freedom, justice, and equality.

Chapter Overview

So that the reader can better comprehend the four tenets of womanist ethics, each chapter of this text outlines methods that will be explored for the fleshing out of these aforementioned tenets of womanist ethics, both for their theoretical applications and practical value. Each thematic chapter focusing on womanist ethical approaches to literary analysis, sociological analysis, and historiography introduces methods that explicate the first three tenets (radical subjectivity, traditional communalism, and redemptive self-love). The fourth tenet, critical engagement, is exemplified through a practical strategy that may be used as a pedagogical tool or exercise.

The first chapter, on literary analysis, takes a close look at the black woman's literary tradition as a valid source for understanding the ethical values black women have created and cultivated in their struggle for survival and self-empowerment. The black woman's literary tradition offers numerous resources for womanist ethicists as it illustrates black women's experiences, serves as a repository of black women's moral wisdom, and becomes the privileged site for the exploration of black female empowerment that would otherwise be overshadowed by the suffering as a result of the forces of white, capitalist, patriarchal systems. Black women's writing is, therefore, a conceptual space where one can imagine what might have been or what was never recorded in any context or form, as well as a model for liberatory praxis. The three methods that will be explored, both for their theoretical applications and practical value, are biomythography (radical subjectivity), virtue ethics (redemptive self-love), and diasporic analysis (traditional communalism).

The second chapter, on sociological analysis, focuses on the study of black women's moral agency and development as it is driven by the need for empirical research to undergird constructive ethics. Sociological analysis mandates scrutinizing factors such as race, class, gender, and religion as key elements of systemic oppression. Research methods gleaned from sociology help womanist ethics to illustrate the multidimensional aspects of how black women come to understand themselves, families, communal living, cultural values, and religious practices within the context of those selfsame systems. The three methods and practices under consideration here — the dance of redemption (redemptive self-love), case study analysis (traditional communalism), and emancipatory metaethnography (radical subjectivity) — make visible the oppressive structures that continue to negatively impact black women's lives and the task that these women undertake to overcome the obstacles such structures impose upon them. Through social analysis we can examine contemporary black women's lives in such a way that present negative experiences can be transformed into positive life chances.

The third chapter, on historiography, seeks to debunk the historical accounts about black women and their trials and triumphs by bringing to light those life stories and faith narratives that have been either marginalized or skewed within traditional historical discourse. A historiographical orientation to womanist ethics demystifies history-as-truth by forcing the researcher to come to grips with the real-lived experiences of black women while also compelling her or him to question why these stories were ignored, lost, or simply never recorded. Womanist ethicists frequently use slave narratives, biographies, and autobiographies in order to chart the ways that black women's histories, leadership roles, and activist spirit have historically created communal values and standards. Womanist historiographical approaches to slave narratives (radical subjectivity), moral biography and autobiography (traditional communalism), and emancipatory historiography (redemptive self-love) offer theoretical avenues that reveal how ordinary women were able to carry out extraordinary tasks in the name of social justice.

Practical Strategies for Critical Engagement

At the end of each chapter, I outline a practical womanist strategy for critical engagement. These practical strategies and pedagogical methods challenge dominant intellectual legacies, theological resources, and ideologies that undermine the goals of womanist ethics, namely, the empowerment of black women. Womanist pedagogy includes new justice-praxis strategies that make visible the contributions of black culture by foregrounding personal and collective accountability, and by engaging in a dialogical process that expects both teacher and student to be responsible for studying black culture through the eyes of black women and also for seeing such a study as inextricably intertwined in their own individual moral development. In this way, womanist pedagogy becomes the vehicle for a liberation ethics; it promotes a learning process that calls for structures that would allow all learners to freely express their moral agency.

An Invitation to the Reader

At present womanist ethics is at a crossroads. Since its emergence in academic societies and classrooms of religion and ethics, non–black women scholars and students have heard numerous womanist scholars claim, "No, you can't be a womanist, but you can certainly use [our] methodology!"[10] Yet having no clear guide as to what those methodologies were, many viewed womanism and especially womanist ethics

as little more than an experiential theoretical orientation, academic
clique, or confessional discourse. Though obviously a primer for those
womanist students and scholars, this text also has the non-womanist
in mind. It is written for undergraduate students, seminarians, and
graduate students in religion as well as for those faculty seeking to
re-tool in womanist approaches to religion and ethics in general. It is
an ideal companion for reading and understanding works written by
and/or about black women, including fiction or nonfiction, academic
or popular texts. *Mining the Motherlode* is also a sourcebook — one
that scholars, religious leaders, practitioners, activists, and students
alike, regardless of gender, race, or class, may find valuable as they
engage in work with, for, and about black women and the larger task
of liberation ethics.

I offer this text as an outgrowth of my work as a student, teacher,
and scholar of womanist ethics and not as pure distillation of the
scholarship of pioneering womanist ethicists. Instead, I seek to affirm
the often undiscerned methodological contributions of these womanist scholars by replicating, extrapolating, or using models that I have
witnessed in their work and show how these invaluable gems of intellectual insight have greatly enriched my own ethical analysis and
that of countless others. Thus, if the reader derives any benefits from
Mining the Motherlode, it should be found in the ways I attempt to construct a layered framework in order to isolate, indicate, and illuminate
in a systematic fashion both the methodological structure and moral
content within the work of black women scholars of religion. In this
sense, I hope to celebrate the existing womanist scholarship and also
help propel the current enterprise of womanist ethics further ahead.

Chapter One

Black Women's Literary Analysis as a Source for Constructive Womanist Ethics

Black women writers function as continuing symbolic conveyors and transformers of the values acknowledged by the female members of the black community. In the quest for appreciating black women's experience, nothing surpasses the black women's literary tradition. It cryptically records the specificity of the Afro-American life.[1]

The black women's literary tradition is a valid source for understanding how ethical values are created and cultivated in an individual or communal struggle for survival and empowerment. One may wonder why black women's writings should be privileged as a site that represents black reality when in fact it is regarded and names itself as fiction. How can fiction reflect reality? More particularly, why is it important to analyze women's literature as a resource for constructive ethics?

Womanists and black feminists have long contended that black women's writings should not be regarded merely as fiction — that is, art for art's sake — but rather as a researched response to black women's socioethical experiences in the face of a history of oppression. Womanist Karen Baker-Fletcher asserts this perspective when she states that "black women's literature is narrative and narrative is essentially an interpretive construction of perceptions of truth through myth and history."[2] Black women's writing particularly represents the real-life experiences of black women's oppression. Referred to by Saunders Redding as a "literature of necessity," black women's literary tradition is utilitarian in nature because it provides a venue of expression to those communal voices that would otherwise be silenced or distorted within dominant literary representations and the perspectives on the realities of the black community that these representations transmit as "truth."[3] This particular function of black women's literary tradition renders it a critical resource for womanist ethics inasmuch as it foregrounds the moral exigencies and ethical perspectives of those severely disadvantaged by racial, sexual, and economic discrimination. This womanist assessment of black women's writing as truth-telling is not a fortuitous recognition; on the contrary, black women writers themselves have understood this as the primary intention driving their writing. As Zora Neale Hurston states in a letter to Langston Hughes:

> For I not only want to present the material with all the life and color of my people, I want to leave no loopholes for the scientific crowd to rend and tear us. I am leaving the story material almost untouched. I have only tampered with it where the story teller was not clear. I know it is going to read different, but that is the glory of the thing, don't you think?[4]

Black scholars have long attested to the importance of black women's literature as a textual site that captures the experiences of black communal life. They have further noted that the saliency of the black women's literary tradition lies not in its ability to catalogue narratives of black life that run counter to the stereotypes imposed by white society. Instead, its saliency derives from its critique of the very systems and ideologies that created such stereotypes, as well as in its production of a constructive moral ethic that creates a more complex and diverse representation of black communal life. Black female religious scholars in particular have found in this tradition an inspiration for critical inquiry into the nature of institutional forms of domination, as bell hooks has observed:

> Black women writers have been a courageous vanguard fictively exploring various politics of domination in black life — racism, sexism, and capitalism — and questioning institutions religious and secular that reinforce and uphold these structures. Their writing necessarily inspires black women scholars attempting to create new critical direction. *Within theology, black women scholars have been among the most willing to acknowledge this supportive influence, identifying it as one of many traditions shaping their theoretical perspectives* [my emphasis].[5]

Womanist ethicists in particular have been pioneers in their efforts to use black women's literature as a source for shaping new theoretical perspectives for gleaning ethical sources that reflect and enhance the reality of black communal life. Katie G. Cannon, the progenitor of womanist ethics, has been the leader in culling from black women writers' literary texts the sacred values and ethical norms reflective of the community's sociocultural practices. She justifies as follows that the black women's literary tradition is a privileged source for her own exploration of womanist ethics:

> The Black woman's literary tradition delineates the many ways that ordinary Black women have fashioned value patterns and ethical procedures in their own terms, as well as mastering, transcending, radicalizing and sometimes destroying pervasive, negative orientations imposed by the mores of the larger society.[6]

Once Cannon opened up this pathway in her work, other womanist theologians and ethicists followed.[7] "[B]ecause it preserves much of the moral wisdom of Black-folk culture and a survival ethic that has been transmitted through an oral/aural tradition,"[8] the womanist tradition in religion redirects black women's scholarship within the academy of religion as a vital source for theological ethics.

In examining black women's literature as a repository of moral wisdom in which the female characters have subverted racist, sexist, and classist ideologies we may come to some understanding of the degree to which literature helps record, imagine, and aid women in their journey toward moral agency.

Marking the Differences:
Black Feminist Literary and Womanist Ethics Orientations to the Black Women's Literary Tradition

Black feminist literary criticism and womanist ethicists' analyses of literary texts are analogous inasmuch as they both seek to correct damaging and dehumanizing stereotypes of black women while celebrating the resilience of African American culture in general, and women's culture in particular. Yet, though these orientations share a common vision by drawing on black women's writings as a source for articulating an identity politics that defines black women's varied experiences, they are divergent in both their methodological means and theoretical ends.

Black feminist criticism emerged as a response to the radical writings of young black women novelists of the 1960s and 1970s, who had begun to produce works that foregrounded the experiences of black women through space and time. These works were deemed subversive. Both black women writers and the critics who highlighted their work were considered radical because either through fiction or criticism they rewrote history and forced the American imagination to wrestle with the atrocities of American society, from enslavement to Jim and Jane Crow segregation. At the same time, they were celebrating the beauty and power of black culture, as evidenced in the Harlem Renaissance, civil rights movement, Black Power, and the Black Arts movement — movements that had all survived in spite of the deleterious effects of a racist, sexist, and classist American legacy. Black feminist literary

critics have focused on the ways in which these women writers deliberately shattered the stereotypes of black women, who were caught in
a mammy-villain representation within the white and/or male imagination. Leading black literary feminist Barbara Christian crystallizes
the power of this new canon formation:

> By the mid-seventies, Afro-American women fiction writers,
> like Paule Marshall, Toni Morrison, Alice Walker, Toni Cade
> Bambara and Gayl Jones, had not only defined their cultural
> context as a distinctly Afro-American one, but they had also
> probed many of the facts of the interrelationship of sexism and
> racism in their society. Not only had they demonstrated the
> fact that sexism existed in black communities, but they had also
> challenged the prevailing definition of woman in American so-
> ciety, especially in relation to motherhood and sexuality. And
> they had insisted not only on the centrality of black women to
> Afro-American history, but also on their pivotal significance to
> present-day social political developments in America.[9]

Black feminist literary critics such as Christian helped to usher in a
new genre of literary criticism, one that showcased the writings of
black women and included them among the treasured works of great
American literature.

In contrast to the aforementioned goals of black feminist literary
criticism, in particular its reevaluation of the literary canon in its gendered, raced, and class dimensions, the womanist ethical trajectory
is not one that has literary criticism as its means or end. Rather,
womanist ethicists turn to literature in order to better perceive the
ultimate concern of women in their moral agency formation. Simply
put, whereas literary criticism on black women's writing is *reflective*
of the ways in which black women writers understand and re-present
their sociohistorical realities and identity formation, womanist ethicists deem black women's texts as *constructive* paradigms of moral

wisdom. Womanist scholar of religion Joy Browne states as follows in an African American analysis of literature:

> the literary critic and theologian play roles that are at once complementary and circular. In a sense, they are working with the same material — African-American culture and society, with all the complexities and idiosyncrasies born of a peculiar history in the United States.... The African-American literary critic takes the "text" of the culture — be it literature, "orature," or event — and decodes the content encoded in language, structure, style, and context: What does this text really *say* to us? What does it *not* say? The theologian takes the same material and examines its content for issues of meaning and ultimate significance: What does this text really *mean* for my life? What does it imply about my humanity, as one made and formed in the image of God?[10]

Womanist religious ethicists attend to black women's writings as sacred texts because embedded within them is a strong tradition of charting the crux of black women's spirituality — their persistent questioning of theodicy, their spiritual strivings, and their radically immanent concepts of the divine.[11] From these sacred texts, womanist ethicists carve out a new canon, a veritable storehouse of life stories that illuminate the experiences of survival and liberation in the midst of evil and suffering. Seeing them as one and the same thing, the womanist ethicist's literary agenda attends to both the theological problem of evil and suffering as sin and the social problem of tripartite oppression as systemic injustice. In this regard, womanist ethical literary methods provide exegetical analyses of black women's sacred texts in order to render theoretical prescriptions for both social criticism and theological reflection. More significantly, womanist ethicists glean from these texts prophetic models of liberation enacted by the female characters as strategies of resistance for addressing the questions of agency, relationships, and quests for liberation.

Thus, black women's writings serve as a valuable medium through which a womanist ethical-centered critique can be formed as an alternative to the marginalization resulting from the canonical, theological, and philosophical sources that are usually employed in normative Christian ethics. A womanist ethical analysis of literature is necessary in order to complete what the fields of literary criticism and normative Christian ethics have left undone, namely the creation of a knowledge base that carves out truths and meanings appropriate to our understanding of the best representation of human virtue and who can embody it. In what follows I explore three womanist ethical-centered methods that use black women's literary work both for their theoretical applications and practical value: (1) biomythography (radical subjectivity), (2) virtue ethics (redemptive self-love), and (3) diasporic analysis (traditional communalism). These methods have been used, as I show, to revise our understanding of the moral formation of black women's writings as sacred texts in their own right for constructive ethics that in turn can effect a canonical transformation within the guilds of literary criticism and ethics.

Biomythography

Biomythography, a term first coined by Audre Lorde in her personal testimony, *Zami*, is a "deliberate amalgamation of autobiographical fact and mythically resonant fiction" that locates the struggle for moral agency and self-identity in a context of social oppression.[12] Through the process of analyzing biomythography, womanist ethicists decode the social ills that black women have internalized within the fabric of their lives. Womanists refer to and explore black women's literature in order to unearth the moral chronicles of black women by transforming orality into a written rendering of this ongoing process of conscientization. In turn, this allows for the understanding of the self that exists separate and apart from the objectified position one holds in society. As Lorde notes in her biomythographical journey, it is necessary for black women to delve into the effects that internalized oppression have had on their inability to be agents of their own destiny. She underscores this by stating that the ambivalent nature that causes double consciousness is the point at which black women are more focused on that which oppresses them than having their own sense of personal power to challenge or recognize that force.

Biomythography allows for the transformation of something that is initially crippling to become something empowering. As literary critic Hortense Spillers notes: "The fact of domination *is* alterable only to the extent that the dominated subject recognizes [her] potential power.... The subject is certainly seen, but she or he certainly sees. It is this latter seeing that negotiates at every point a space for living."[13] Lorde's biomythographical narrative reflects this process of self-recognition through the act of remembering. Feminist theorist Drucilla Cornell nuances the ways in which the self is constructed through remembering when she states, "The recollection of oneself is always an act which imagines through the remembrance of its own claims of selfhood what can never be fully recollected but only forever reimagined and re-told."[14]

In this process of retrospective self-analysis, biomythography, as a preliminary method toward a liberative ethic, calls for a personal narrative that resonates with the genre of autobiography in that it incorporates historical personal facts. However, its unique form transcends such strict objective parameters because higher truths may emerge where historical fact might not be present. Black women's fiction can be read as an unapologetic attempt to bridge the gaps of history by recording what has been disremembered and unacknowledged. Dismissing the Aristotelian distinction between that which was (history) versus that which ought to be (fiction), black women writers, as Toni Morrison notes, should be considered as "the truest of historians."[15]

As a truth-teller, the black woman writer uses language to make concrete and real the reified and abstract notion of history while simultaneously giving flesh and form to real-lived experiences that have been written out of history and obliterated from our own consciousnesses. The biomythographical narrative is a purposeful form of call and response from one unique black woman's voice to a larger community of women who are invited to resonate with her voice and become a part of it. These women, when coming together into this new mythic community, become transformed. Womanist literary scholar Carolyn Medine calls this interaction "multivocality," a "translation across boundaries" that involves risk taking and dexterity: "the writer risks to take this role and to translate — to incorporate, embody — it into story and thereby draws us to it: this altar at which all utterance is a present act."[16] The experiences of the collective body, within this new context, inform a greater truth about women than could be reflected by any of their individual identities taken separately.

Arguably, biomythography represents the textual counterpart to the African cosmological term, *nommo*. Whereas Afrocentric theorist Molefi Asante defines *nommo* as "the generative and productive power of the spoken word," the womanist ethicist may deem biomythography as its narrative equivalent.[17] In the act of recording lost memories, the woman writer properly names and gives essence to what is caught at the crossroads of history (that which is hidden but recovered) and myth (that which is created and/or discovered). This sentiment is epitomized by Medine, who underscores the role of the facilitator of the embodied testimony as a "translator" of thoughts that have never been thought or spoken, because they are too terrifying:

It is the writer who can speak the name we fear to speak. What the translator of the name, the one ... who searches and finds lost things, does is to think the thinking through which the thought is thought, thereby enacting the thought. She, then, draws the thought into her own voice, saying what others refuse to say — indeed, what has never yet been said — in her own voice.[18]

Biomythography is a method that is well suited for the task of charting black women's radical subjectivity, the first tenet of womanist ethics, making it not just a mere description but rather a developmental process that can be reproduced. The purpose of this womanist ethical method of literary analysis is to trace the process of radical subjectivity as identity formation and personal empowerment through five stages: *(1) articulation of embodied testimony, (2) re-memory of disremembered memories, (3) demythologizing of normative ideologies, (4) interrogation of internalized oppression, and (5) remythologizing of life story.*

Articulation of Embodied Testimony: Telling without Tampering

Embedded within black women's writings are testimonies that witness to the embodied experiences of individual black women who find themselves on a journey toward self-discovery amidst socials ills that seek to name, define, and circumscribe their self-definition. Such embodied testimony resonates with the black church ritual of witnessing to the congregation of believers how God has kept and restored them in the midst of trials and tribulations. In doing what is often referred to as "telling the truth and shaming the devil," the act of testifying about one's embodied experience is, as womanist theologian Michele Jacques states, the subjective ground out of which black women's faith tradition and identity formation is nurtured:

> Embedded here are the beliefs that one *must* tell the truth about one's self and one's situation: that this truth *is* the way to freedom either in, through or out of the situation; that any suppression of the truth *is* an evil which fortifies devilish oppression; and ultimately, that this embodied testimony of truth *liberates* the *very* soul of the community.[19]

Jacques underscores the sacred nature of embodied testimony in claiming that the self-revelatory testimony tradition for the black woman "is the altar before which she stands to 'tell the truth' of her embodied presence to a world congregation."[20] In so doing, she liberates herself from her imposed silence by offering her prophetic voice to those within her community "who have an ear to hear."[21]

Biomythographical texts, such as *Zami* and Toni Morrison's *Beloved*, can be considered part of this black testimonial tradition and defy the evil forces that seek to silence black women. The writers of these testimonies tell for the first time the private pains of victims-turned-heroines and the events that have triggered them without tampering with the raw material of human suffering that ultimately imbues the protagonists with a positive identity and self-understanding of their humanity. The embodied testimony can be seen at the moment in which the protagonist articulates her experience of a crucial moral conflict. Here, the central character experiences a cognitive dissonance so profound that she begins to reimagine herself and rewrite her life story so as to rescue herself from a nightmarish end. In both Toni Morrison's *Beloved* and Lorde's *Zami*, the death-dealing effects of history are made flesh through the characters of Sethe and Zami. Morrison and Lorde birth composites of women's life experiences that ultimately take on the mythical dimensions of Beloved and Afrekete. Within Lorde's testimony, the moral conflict begins with a yearning to find her lost self, Zami, and a journey that starts with the love and loss of her mother and all of the other women who she comes to love and lose throughout her life. It culminates in a new understanding of her truer, more cumulative self in the mythic personification of Afrekete. Morrison, for her part, emphasizes the initial process of embodied testimony with Sethe's journey to reconcile herself with the enraged spirit of her dead child that refuses to die. So profound is Sethe's embodied testimony and the moral conflict that triggers it, that it too fashions itself into a mythic other, Beloved. Morrison remarked passionately about this process:

Bit by bit I had been rescuing her from the grave of time and inat-
tention. Her fingernails might be in the first book; face and legs,
perhaps, the second time. Little by little bringing her back into
living life. So that now she comes running when called . . . she is
here now, alive.[22]

Whereas the embodied testimony could be understood as a literary
genre particular to black women's writings, biomythography is crucial in the lives and experiences of black women because it holds
itself in tension with and ultimately contests the ideological underpinnings of racialized historical accounts. In light of this, womanist
ethicists have understood the merit as well as purpose of embodied
testimony as the defining moment that appropriately represents and
accurately names the specificity of black women's oppression along
moral lines. As such, the embodied testimony marks the threshold
through which the ethicist is able to enter the story in order to chart
the first step toward radical subjectivity on the moral map of black
women's agency.

Re-Memory of Disremembered Memories

Whereas the embodied testimony marks the threshold of black
women's experiences and quest for moral agency, the re-memory of
disremembered memories serves as the driving force for the conscientization process. Once moral conflict emerges, the floodgates of
disremembered memories open, and the protagonist is forced to risk
the process of undergoing this retrospective journey. In so doing, the
protagonist creates a ritual space into which others are called forth
to participate, sharing in the re-memory process (recovering what was
once known) by re-membering (bringing together that which has been
taken or torn apart). The exchange of stories is a reflexive act for the
characters who seek to flesh out the conditions under which they
experience and confront oppression.

The embodied stories of other women come to light in response to and converge with the testimony that is told by the black female protagonist, as evidenced in novels like Alice Walker's *The Color Purple* or Gloria Naylor's *The Women of Brewster Place*. These novels reflect the struggles of black women whose identities may differ, but their contexts are the same. Whereas their age, political consciousness, and sexual preference are different, they share the common experience of race, class, and gender oppression. Taken altogether, their exchange of stories corroborates the subjective understanding of the life story the protagonist tells. According to Medine, the womanist scholar's task in charting the re-memory of disremembered memories is to articulate its value as a sacred act wherein black women writers are

> making the space for us to step into and to experience the past — to remember — in our present plane of existence. . . . Re-memory is, as Pilate reminds us in *Song of Solomon* and as Sethe reminds us in *Beloved*, the reality that nothing dies: everything is always now and the dead we kill are ours. The task of the writer is to access memory — "to say it, repeat it" — and, then to replace us in re-memory. In this way, the writer is a kind of hierophant — one who shows — and a holy person — one who creates the ritual space in which we can experience the origin again and become responsible for it.[23]

Baker-Fletcher uses re-memory to excavate from the text the epistemological underpinnings that impact black women's identity formation:

> Like archaeologists, womanist theologians must engage in a process of recovery to examine the fragments of our past. We must engage in what Morrison's characters in *Beloved* refer to as re-memory to recover a full sense of what it means to be created free and equal — to reconstruct Black Womanhood. In order to transform the present social order with its distorted images

of Black Womanhood, we must take into account the depth, richness, and pain of our African heritage. Both mythic and historical ancestors, along with their communities, offer important information for a reconstruction of womanhood.[24]

The responsibility of the ethical analyst here is to focus on the various ways in which re-memory is enacted. Primarily, re-memory is the act of recalling not only the collective testimonies themselves, but also the information revealed within them. Additionally, re-memory brings together seemingly unrelated, secondary stories that are laid out within the text, enjoining them to enter into dialogue with the protagonist's testimony. Also, re-memory is a corrective of a past erroneous belief or perspective — discovering a truth that may have been distorted by the protagonist or by other characters. Ultimately, re-memory can be a means of calling into existence that which has never been said before as though it has always existed in order to glean the moral imperative: to reveal the distortion that has perpetuated black women's pain or oppressive conditions or prevented them from any form of preservation or agency.

Demythologizing of Normative Ideologies

The characters' reactions to the re-memory or re-membering of disremembered memories are, in fact, an awakening to their experiences of oppression that are neither the result of the natural order of things nor consequential to their own actions. The characters begin to derive knowledge of the world around them by assessing their own experiences. They discover that the impetus behind these unchanging and seemingly natural patterns of domination and subjugation are the result of social structures that they had never considered as forces exerting power over their lives.

The ethicist, in noting this phase of the characters' moral development, charts the process by which black women within the text start to home in on the ideologies or myths that hindered them from determining their own identity. The re-memory phase is initiated when the protagonist hears the life stories of her female counterparts. After hearing the testimonies of others, the protagonist begins to wonder whether what she believed to be either a consequence of her own behavior or divinely preordained is actually socially constructed. She comes to see that the consequences impact her life so absolutely that in essence they represent a ubiquitous supernatural force. When she realizes that what has been posed as truth is actually a lie, she seeks clarity. In the process of demystification, the female protagonist decisively confronts theodicy and wrestles to discern what a true sense of divine justice is — that which is yoked with and facilitates social justice. Celie, in Alice Walker's *The Color Purple*, illustrates this process. Celie frees herself from being subjected to silence, shame, and suffering by realizing that God was not a "big and old and tall and graybearded and white" man who was "trifling, forgitful and lowdown." But rather God was something that was inside her and everyone else. This character learns that because of the pervasiveness of the normative gaze of racist and sexist ideologies, demystification is typically a long and ongoing process. Shug explains this to the recently awakened Celie:

> Man corrupt everything, say Shug. He on your box of grits, in your head, and all over the radio. He try to make you think he everywhere. Soon as you think he everywhere, you think he God. But he ain't. Whenever you trying to pray, and man plop himself on the other end of it, tell him to git lost, say Shug. Conjure up flowers, wind, water, a big rock.
>
> But this hard work, let me tell you. He been there so long, he don't want to budge ... conjure up a rock ... throw it.[25]

In reviewing such passages, the ethicist notes how in this particular phase of biomythography, female protagonists such as Celie and Sethe do not push against but rather rise above the social constraints imposed upon them as they tap into a radical subjective power within themselves motivated by their "wanting to know more and in greater depth than is considered 'good' for one."[26] This prophetic critique, as womanist Cheryl Townsend Gilkes affirms, is a form of demystification that is not just a reactive posture to systems of oppression, but rather a force of spirituality that springs from the transformative act of being in charge and taking oneself seriously.[27] As Emilie Townes states in regard to this radically immanent concept of the divine found within black women's literature,

> [This] understanding of the Spirit [is] woven intricately into the very fabric of existence itself... [and] challenges Afro-Americans to explore the profundity of the parenthood of God with its promise-invoking images of birthing and nurturing whole peoples into freedom and wholeness.[28]

Interrogation of Internalized Oppression

In this stage of the biomythographical method, the womanist ethicist examines the ways in which the central female characters begin to see themselves as they gaze through the mirror that the life stories reflect back to them. Adopting a perspective that is equally reflective and reflexive causes them to thoroughly question why they do what they do. The ethicist notes a critical juncture characterized by the protagonists' act of introspection. This becomes evident, first, by the self-questioning of the ways in which they have been complicit in their own oppression and those of others. It later becomes evident by the ways in which the characters affirm themselves, which can be noted in their efforts to free themselves from the structures of racism and sexism in order to define themselves individually as well as who they are in relationship to others in their community. The biomythographical narratives in Maya Angelou's *I Know Why the Caged Bird Sings*, Gwendolyn Brooks's *Maud Martha*, Paule Marshall's *Browngirl, Brownstones*, and Toni Morrison's *Tar Baby* serve as examples of the work of interrogating internalized oppression — that process of critical self-reflexivity

that leads to critical consciousness. In each of these works, the protagonist rejects other people's definitions of who she is, how she looks,
how she should act, and what values and beliefs she should hold.

Remythologizing of Life Story

This last stage of biomythographical method is a cumulative articulation of the protagonist's journey from embodied testimony to radical
subjectivity. Although the central characters in these diverse stories
are neither necessarily triumphant nor defeated upon confronting the
forces that seek to subjugate them, they have engaged in the important process of claiming their own definition of self. As we see in
Gwendolyn Brooks's *Maud Martha*, an ordinary black woman attempts
not only to survive in her subjugated roles as daughter, mother, and
wife, but also to create a context in which she can *audaciously, courageously*, or *willfully* be *responsible, in charge* and *serious* about her own
self-determination. In her analysis of Brooks's classic *Maud Martha*,
literary critic Barbara Christian highlights this ability of the protagonist to remythologize her life story as she liberates her life in the midst
of oppression:

> What Brooks emphasizes in the novel is Maud Martha's "aware-
> ness" that she is seen as common (and therefore as unimportant),
> and that there is so much more in her than her "little life"
> will allow her to be. Yet, because Maud Martha constructs her
> own standards, she manages to transform that "little life" into so
> much more despite the limits set on her by her family, her hus-
> band, her race, her class, whites, and American society.... She
> manages, though barely, to be her own creator.[29]

Baker-Fletcher notes a similar process of demythologizing and
remythologizing in Toni Morrison's *Tar Baby*, in the life of the protagonist Jadine. Baker-Fletcher contends that Jadine has forgotten the
ancient properties of black culture and their application to her current

social circumstance. As a result of this dilemma, the character must learn to nurture and hold things together for her family and culture:

> *Tar baby,* as revisioned myth, reveals that a tar baby shaped by Euro-centric values cannot be a true culture bearer for the African-American Community. At the same time, the original myth uncovers a more profound truth regarding tar's sacred properties in relation to Black Women's ancestral heritage. To image oneself according to western mythos of Black womanhood is to submit to a false, fragmented self-image. To be a true culture bearer and community builder, Black Women must remember the moral wisdom of the ancestors. One such ancestor is the mythological Tar Lady.[30]

By speaking truth to power, reconstructing history, exposing false myths, and refusing to conspire with their own oppression, the female protagonists move from the margins to the center of their own consciousness. Herein they become the creator of their own destiny and the authors of their own myths — in effect, claiming the creative force within themselves, referred to by poet Ntozake Shange with her declaration, "i found god in myself & I loved her / i loved her fiercely."

In this phase, the female protagonists' agency lies in their ability to imagine themselves beyond how they are regarded by those around them. In this radical revisioning, they carve out a way of knowing and being that exists in spite of and counter to any other system or structure that seeks to define or circumscribe them.

The womanist ethicist, in this phase of biomythographical method, charts: the stance and the stage of rebelliousness of the characters and determines to what extent their consciousness has been altered; the quality of their commitment to establishing a new vision for life outside of the parameters of normative ideologies and the social constraints such ideologies impose upon them; and the paths by which their internal contradictions are dissolved. Thus, through these five steps, radical subjectivity can be understood not only as the moral formative stages as they are named, but also the emergent spiritual acts that result from each stage: testifying, telling the truth, and shaming the devil; making ritual space and doing holy acts; confronting evil forces with supernatural power; drawing on ancestral properties; and radically transforming oneself into the image of God.

Virtue Ethics

While biomythography represents black women's audacious attempts to claim their agency through the attainment of radical subjectivity, virtue ethics continues this moral formation development by focusing on the third womanist ethical tenet: the redemptive project of self-love as identity politics and self-actualization. Black women's identity politics serves as a standard for what it means to be a virtuous person in the face of insurmountable adversity. Simply put, whereas biomythography allows womanist ethicists to map the process of black women's agency, virtue ethics is a method that allows womanist ethicists to ascertain the particularities of black women's moral character.

According to Aristotelian ethics and modern moral philosophy, virtue is defined as whatever characteristic or personal quality that manifests within an observer a sense of satisfaction and liking toward a particular trait of an individual. Vice is its antithesis. In normative terms, people who are discerned as virtuous are those whose traits are perceived as useful. One's desirable character (value) is linked to and renders a desired practical end (use). Portrayed as such, normative ethics portends a dominant perspective that assumes that both the observer and observed are self-directing agents possessing freedom and a wide range of choices therein. Within this perspective, every moral agent, whether observer or observed, possesses both the agency and the means to achieve desired ends that would allow them to be considered virtuous. For example, Emilie Townes argues that "[d]ominant ethics makes a virtue of qualities that lead to economic success: self-reliance, frugality, and industry...and it can make suffering a desirable norm."[31]

As Townes indicates, normative ethics arrests the process of logic and moral reasoning for those whose social circumstances preclude economic success, in spite of their frugality and daily suffering. Pushing against this universalizing framework for understanding virtue, more recent debates within moral philosophical theory contend that virtue-based theories must address the particularities of specific communities.[32] Addressing the specificity of the black moral experience, Cannon argues:

> In the African American community, the aggregate of the qualities that determine desirable ethical values regarding the uprightness of character and soundness of moral conduct must always take into account the circumstances, paradoxes, and the dilemmas that constrict Blacks to the lowest range of self-determination.[33]

In this vein, womanist ethics argues that communities of the dispossessed (people of color, white women, poor people, and other marginalized groups) are not afforded equal opportunities to achieve social freedom nor economic success relative to their white male counterparts. Similarly, whereas the "universalizing" virtues of industry and suffering may be self-directing means that bring about desired ends for members of the privileged class, these attributes do not result in the desired ends of success or freedom for members of communities of the dispossessed. Indeed, a double standard is imposed, because what is seen as virtuous for the privileged class is considered vice when endured by the non-privileged.

Normative ethics and its Eurocentric and patriarchal paradigms of theological and moral virtue have dismissed and/or devalued black women's experience, humanity, and character. Such moral discourse extends these domains only to those who enjoy white and/or male privilege. Due to the interlocking systems of race, class, and gendered oppression, black women in particular are denied the right to appear as good or virtuous. A womanist analysis of virtue corrects such limiting definitions, ones that disfigure black women's moral character as essentially lacking in virtue. As Cannon states with reference to the histories of enslavement, colonization, and Jane Crow segregation, virtue "is the moral wisdom that women of African ancestry live out in their existential context which does not appeal to the fixed rules or absolute principles of the white-oriented, male-structured society."[34]

Departing from a more particularized framework for understanding virtue, a womanist method of virtue ethics entails an analysis of the contexts of oppression within black women's writing in which the moral character development of black women is birthed and nurtured. To develop a fully actualized sense of moral character and thus wrest one's agency from the annihilating forces of oppression is to cultivate a peculiar wisdom that does not resonate with Eurocentric, patriarchal, or elitist sensibilities and systemic structures. The task of the womanist ethicist here is to chart within the black female literary canon the moral wisdom of surviving and thriving in the face of oppression and the coping strategies that emerge out of their struggle for redemptive self-love.

Black women's literature depicts the contours of the moral sphere of black women's virtue by illustrating the multivalent survival mechanisms used and developed by black women in order to redeem as virtuous what has been considered vice. According to Cannon,

> the Black woman's literary tradition provides a rich resource and a cohesive commentary that brings into sharp focus the Black community's central values, which in turn frees Black folk from the often deadly grasp of these parochial stereotypes.[35]

Cannon, the leading scholar of womanist virtue ethics, interrogates literature as a site for doing this method of constructive ethics. Cannon names and defines what has been classically referred to as the

exemplary tenets of womanist virtue, found not only within black
women writers' lives but also within that of their female literary
counterparts. In her pioneering work, *Black Womanist Ethics*, Cannon outlines and defines three subaltern womanist virtues that can be
gleaned from black women's writings: *invisible dignity, quiet grace,* and
unshouted courage.

According to Cannon's womanist theory of virtue, *invisible dignity*
is black women's self-celebration and self-survival in the midst of adversity. In the onslaught of stereotypes and mockery, black women
maintain their sense of who they are as both good and virtuous in
their literal and figurative embodiment of "culture bearer" (loves her
culture — music, dance, moon, love, roundness, folk). Cheryl Kirk-
Duggan further argues that a womanist virtue ethic posits that the
attributes that make black women easy targets for ridicule and oppression do not in fact succeed in turning them into victims.[36] To the
contrary, those attempts that are made to render them powerless only
serve to foster within them a critical apparatus that empowers them to
work creatively within and oftentimes transcend oppressive systems.
This has been noted throughout the history of African American oppression. Enslaved Africans used "a theology of ingenuity" in which
they understood God as a "way-maker," a theology that empowered
them to take what they were given and make of it what they wanted
and needed. This moral and divinely inspired wisdom has been a mainstay within black women's identity politics. Their ability to finesse the
common and base aspects of society in addition to making something
noble and valuable of them is the gift of black women's moral wisdom.
The redemptive creativity of black women's moral wisdom underlies
and informs the third tenet of womanist ethics, that of redemptive
self-love.

The second womanist virtue within Cannon's theory is *quiet grace*.
Quiet grace is the self-knowledge of black women that operates as
functional prudence — the search for truth. Having its roots in the
gift of discernment that emanates from the *love* of the Spirit and

love of the Folk, quiet grace has both spiritual and social features. As an unadulterated expression of folk wisdom, quiet grace is a quest to exercise judicious forethought in negotiating what is socially considered legitimate versus what black people know in fact to be true and palpable to their day-to-day realities. As divine wisdom, quiet grace invokes spiritual discernment as a means to aid black women in distinguishing satanic forces from divine will and righteousness from iniquity. As the foundation of identity politics, quiet grace is not a confrontational opposition of one person's truth over another's. Rather, Cannon characterizes quiet grace "as looking at the world with one's own eyes, forming judgments and demythologizing whole bodies of so-called social legitimacy."[37]

The third womanist virtue that Cannon highlights as central to black women's identity politics is *unshouted courage*. Unshouted courage is a virtue that has as its center a sense of unctuousness and self-affirmation. Unshouted courage highlights the quality of black women's steadfastness and fortitude in the face of tyranny. Cannon makes this point as follows:

> Unshouted courage is a virtue evolving from the forced responsibility of black women. In its basic sense, it means the quality of steadfastness, akin to fortitude, in the face of formidable oppression. The communal attitude is far more than "grin and bear it." Rather, it involves the ability to "hold on to life" against major opposition.[38]

Unshouted courage thus evokes the womanist sentiment of *loves the struggle* in that it upholds black women's feistiness about life. In spite of attempts to malign their character or subjugate their selfhood, black women overcome those social forces that attempt to wipe out their intrinsic will to *love themselves regardless*.

By and large, black women's writings are such a critical resource for the study of virtue ethics because great attention is paid to the specificity of black people's experiences in America within the black literary tradition. As Cannon notes, black women's writings are in-formed not by the personal values of the author. Rather, this literature is a testament to the values of the black community writ large, within designated time frames and contexts.[39] As culture bearers in their own right, black women writers not only chronicle the histories of black people within the context of tripartite oppression but also illumine the social ethos and the religious ethics that convey their values in the face of such realities. Furthermore, womanist ethicists and theolo-gians have noted that black women's writings epitomize such a nexus of ethos and ethics inasmuch as their female characters embody self-love in both their human and divine dimensions. According to Gilkes, "This love is the greatest issue in human existence and the critical point of convergence between [their] creative thinking and the task of Christian ethics."[40]

The womanist ethical tenet of redemptive self-love is a critical con-tribution to the task of Christian ethics in light of virtue theory. In some classical strains of Christian ethics (Aristotelian), there exist two branches of virtues: intellectual virtue, such as prudence, and moral virtue, such as fortitude. An exemplary virtuous person would pos-sess the mind and the will necessary to both *know* and *do* the right thing. Virtue (excellence as a human being) is thus seen as a state of deliberate moral purpose consisting in a standard that is relative to one's second nature. Such moral standards are determined by reason and will. Whereas this classical tradition does look at and address the thought/action binary logic central to intellectual versus moral virtue, it fails to wrestle with the theological foundation upon which one's thinking and doing rests: the *imago Dei* as evidenced in one's very being. Such a foundation is at the very core of the inquiry of Chris-tian ethics. In order to answer the Christian ethical query of why people do what they do, the task is not to assume a causal dynamic in which thoughts lead universally to moral actions. Instead, this third dimension of a theological virtue (being) intervenes, disrupting nor-mative binary thinking, and making visible the foundational role that identity (who one is) plays in one's thoughts (what one thinks) and actions (what one does).

Indeed, doing virtuous things or thinking virtuously is not necessarily conclusive of one's moral virtue. Rather, one who is virtuous will do these things because it is their very nature. That is to say actions or thoughts (whether random or deliberate) are not evidence of a person's virtue by themselves alone but must be judged in tandem to truly get a sense of a person's essence and/or being. The undermining of the causal dynamic that drives Western (read Eurocentric) binary logic is reversed by the introduction of the third term of "being" that is and should be the departure point for ethics as posited by womanists. Thus, womanist virtue ethics attends to the being-thinking-doing trajectory in order to discern what one should do and how one should think when who one is by one's very nature is considered to be morally bankrupt. The excellence of black women's virtue, not only for studying the moral formation of black women in particular, but also as a contribution to the field of Christian virtue ethics in general, resides in its ability to address moral character along the being-thinking-doing continuum.

Invisible Dignity as Moral Virtue

The moral virtue of invisible dignity is depicted within black women's writings as an ontological self-preservation and celebration of the sanctity of black women's identity amidst oppression. Whether examining poetry, prose, or novels, one is struck by a resonant pattern found in the development of black women's narratives whereby a conversion usually occurs for the character. What from the outset seems to be a near loss of ontological security, the narrative's conclusion results in a journey that leads the black female protagonists to the redemption of self-love and a truer sense of humanity. The moral essence of black womanhood is extracted from misrecognitions and misrepresentations of her moral character. Following Cannon's womanist literary analysis model, in order to chart the moral situation of black women and their quest for self-preservation and celebration of moral character, the womanist ethicist's first task is to pose some essential questions about the text: *How does this source portray blackness, darkness, and economic justice for non-ruling-class people? What are women doing in this text? Are they infantilized, put on pedestals, idealized — or allowed to be free and independent?*[41] The task of the womanist ethicists to determine if moral virtue aligns itself with or is opposed to the representation of blackness and womanhood in the text, if this positioning evolves over time, and how the author positions the reader with respect to the moral dilemma that such alignments or misrepresentations pose.

There are several examples in black women's literature of female characters who are enthralled by the controlling stereotypes and insidious images that often plague black women. As Janie reminds us in *Their Eyes Were Watching God*, as Lutie reminds us in *The Street*, as Pauline reminds us in *Contending Forces*, and as Pecola reminds us in *The Bluest Eye*, virtue is something that is not normally associated with darkness, femaleness, and poverty. As Hazel Carby explains, "Black womanhood was polarized against white womanhood."[42] While white women have been regarded as feminine and chaste, virginal and virtuous, black women have been regarded as "the mules of the world," "matriarchs," "superwomen," "mean and evil bitches," "castraters," "Sapphires," and "mammies." The task of the womanist ethicist is to unpack the hidden virtue found within blackness and femaleness by recognizing the black female protagonists' reflection on and formulation of their own self-worth, unfettered by the normative assessment of black women as lacking moral virtue.

In order to decode how blackness and darkness are portrayed, the notion of colorism is key. Particular physicality and aesthetics are ascribed particular levels of virtue. For instance, Western aestheticism suggests that lighter shades of black are considered beautiful and thereby virtuous. Yet the great irony is that lighter or whiter skin within the black community is most likely a product of sexual violence by whites. We can see evidence of this practice in black women's writings like Gayl Jones's *Corregidora*. In *Corregidora*, we find the protagonist Ursa questioning the cost-benefit ratio of her color as a descendant of a Portuguese seaman turned plantation owner who raped her grandmother. Knowing that the tendency of the white and black communities was to find beauty in lighter skin, normatively, Ursa might be tempted to celebrate her lightness and use it as currency to secure for herself a sense of idealized or superior femininity or simply to move up to a higher social class. But rather than cash in on her color currency, she realizes that her color is the embodied evidence of the violation of black women's virtue at the hands of white male slave owners' desires. She realizes that her skin color is the product of a legacy of rape, a legacy of white supremacist ideology, which is based first and foremost on the white degradation and control of black bodies. Paradoxically, rather than reinforce the cultural capital of her skin color, Ursa's evaluation of it ran counter to both normative teleology (goals) and deontology (standards) of Western culture.

In order to chart invisible dignity, then, it is critical to debunk the interlocking systems of race, class, and gender oppression and the ways they incarnate themselves in the lives of the characters who face moral conflict primarily because of the particular characteristics they embody. Here, ethical analysis must be attentive to the economic status of the darkest woman, the social privilege of the lightest or whitest woman, and the ways in which the level of privilege of these differently positioned female protagonists are contested within the text. What the analysis must chart is the redemptive journey of the female protagonist that begins when she is represented as deprived of moral virtue due to her embodied attributes and that ends when the protagonist develops a new sense of self-regard. The reader might initially observe the protagonist's journey with a normative gaze that is affixed to a hierarchical standard of moral virtue; however, by shifting the focus to prioritize the character's self-regard, the normative gaze is later inverted and replaced by an oppositional gaze, wherein the actions and behavior of the protagonist become the sole standard by which her morality is measured.

Quiet Grace as Intellectual Virtue

Quiet grace is a process of clarifying norms in which black women come to redeem their intrinsic value by unearthing who they are. In the process of such reflective self-analysis, black women strip away those external social forces that formed them within the context of tripartite oppression. This search for truth is driven by functional prudence, which strives for immediate survival and potential liberation. The protagonists' journey in black women's literature is fundamentally a search for truth. In it, black female characters "look at the world with their own eyes, form their own judgments and demythologize whole bodies of so-called social legitimacy."[43]

Generally speaking, black women writers and their literary heroines acknowledge the vulnerability they face in attempting to survive in a context that looks upon them with contempt and irreverence. As Cannon states, "The white, elitist attributes of passive gentleness and an enervative delicacy, considered particularly appropriate to womanhood, proved to be non-functional in the pragmatic survival lifestyle of Black women."[44] To emphasize this point, the modifier "quiet" in "quiet grace" is critical because it acknowledges that which has not been articulated about black women's moral character in the face of oppression.

The first task of the ethicist in mapping quiet grace as an intellectual virtue is to *identify and define the mode of oppression*. Here, the ethicist must target the particular form of oppression that manifests itself within the text. It is not enough to simply note that the character is suffering at the hands of some system of injustice; it must be identified in order to attack it. For example, suggesting that Ursa (*Corregidora*), Pecola (*The Bluest Eye*) or Maud Martha (*Maud Martha*) are victims of racism is true — but what particular kind of racism is it?

In what context is it occurring? What privileges or oppressions ensue? For example, colorism is experienced in a quite different manner intraracially versus interracially. Shades of blackness have perennially denoted standards of political citizenship, economic privilege, social opportunity, aesthetic beauty, and most important, moral value within modern society and culture. Within an intraracial context, the blackest woman is destined to be the least valued, regardless of her actions, by means of her color and not simply her race. We see in Gwendolyn Brooks's *Maud Martha*, Dorothy West's "Mammy," and Toni Morrison's Pecola in *The Bluest Eye* the divisive hierarchy that colorism causes even between differently shaded blacks within the same family. These hierarchies and splits occur, moreover, within the very psyches of black women, threatening to distort the sense of self that these women try to cultivate.

The second step in quiet grace is to *locate causes of pervasive cultural racism and manufactured patriarchalism, especially ecclesial clericalization and hierarchalization.* In this stage, it is necessary to chart the progression of oppression that the general malaise of cultural racism contributes, in cumulative fashion, to other interlocking forms of oppression in the lives of black women. In that regard, "cultural racism" is the devaluing of anything that is black. "Manufactured patriarchalism" is the devaluing of anything that is female, whereas "ecclesial clericalization and hierarchalization" represent the religious authority and sacred rhetoric that justifies the perpetuation of them both — resulting in the sanctification of black women's oppression. In light of this, the plight of black womanhood is simply regarded as what is ordained by God. So the ethicist poses essential questions, such as: *How do racism and sexism transform black women's virtues into vices? How do religious mandates and God-talk undergird this subversion, legitimating the denigration and subjugation of black women?* Or, as Karen Baker-Fletcher puts it, "What does it mean to be human in relation to God and the world when one is Black and female?"[45]

The task of the ethicist is to study the religious exhortations, sermons, and pleas that are made in these passages, looking for the ways in which all that is black and female is stereotyped and maligned. Zora Neale Hurston's *Mules and Men*, Alice Walker's *The Color Purple*, and Arthenia J. Bates Millican's *The Deity Nodded* exemplify the ignominious circumstances that black women must face at the hands of an alienating God who has preordained their seemingly miserable fate. For example, the ethicist would look at how Hurston's character George Thomas in *Mules and Men* epitomizes such maligning as he articulates his understanding of God's creation of black women: "She could have had mo' sense, but she told God no, she'd ruther take it out in hips. So God gave her her ruthers. She got plenty hips, plenty mouf and no brains."[46] Focusing on such examples, the ethicist can study the ways in which the vocality and roundness of black women are being maligned. Indeed, women here are shown as not being treated unjustly but rather in a just fashion, getting from God precisely what they deserve and, in fact, in this case what they have asked for. In this sense, God-talk is used to legitimate women's inferiority.

The third step in quiet grace is to *explore the intellectual breadth, conceptual depth, and structural linkage of domination and oppression in their communal manifestations, both domestic and international.* In this step, the analysis focuses on how oppression has become both systemic and pervasive; it affects not only the female protagonist but other people in the local and global community. Domination and suppression are so woven into the fabric of society that society itself defines moral virtue (namely, truth, knowledge, beauty, character, and aesthetic and cultural ideals) in such a way that it is comprehensible only to the oppressors and virtually incomprehensible to the oppressed. Thus, whatever adverse results or circumstances emerge from such interlocking systemic oppressions that are orchestrated in larger societal structures become exponentially and intimately experienced within the black community. It is therefore critical that the black community examine the systemic effects of oppression in light of the fact that "what happens to one can happen to all."[47] Whatever the black female protagonist experiences will instantly impact negatively upon the moral development and quality of life for the black community at large.

As the literary narrative continually reminds us, the black female protagonist's journey and wrestling with systemic forces of oppression do not exist in a vacuum. Rather, they illuminate the moral conflict and social demise that the entire black community must endure and at the same time how the racist effect that one individual endures has a ripple effect on others within the community: intergenerationally, across genders, families, and localities. Here, the system of injustice serves in some twist of irony as a fitting match to the African proverb of "I am because we are" because the symbiotic effects of one individual's experience with oppression finds itself exacerbated as it permeates the community in its entirety.

Jones's *Corregidora* exemplifies this intricate interweaving of the individual's and the community's plight with the devastating effects of cultural racism coupled with sexual exploitation as a stark denunciation of racism and sexism in both white and black communities. By way of illustration, Ursa's light skin is evidence of rape and miscegenation that, although marked on an epidermal level, has had a ripple effect across generations of black progeny. The devastating effects of the sexual violence continually meted out to Ursa's great-grandmother reproduces itself intracommunally, evidenced in Ursa's light skin. This legacy of embodied and embedded violence in the lives of black women represents several injuries to the black community. Not only does Ursa's light skin serve as nonverbal testimony to the legacy of rape and miscegenation, but even darker-skinned women whose complexion reveals no evidence of such a violation are and have been nonetheless violated by such acts. The implications of

Jones's imagery are that the horrors of sexual abuse might in fact be a form of kinship for black women across generations. Moreover, darker-skinned black women suffer further indignity once they realize that Ursa, being more white, is ascribed greater value among black men than they are. Whether consciously or not, this causes the darker-skinned women in the text to ostracize her. The whole community fights both past and present simultaneously because of systems of domination based on one violent act. As Jones's text reveals, these hegemonic structures are created in such fashion as to target the psyches and conditions of individual people and entire communities over space and time in order to make virtually impossible the discernment of its social construction and its roots.

The fourth step of quiet grace is to *see whether the passage aids the victims in overcoming victimization*. In that African American women's literature seeks to demystify those oppressive structures that subjugate both black women and their community, there is also a search for truth that calls for the protagonist's ability to implement a functional prudence that will enable her to rise above oppression's detrimental effects. According to Cannon, the search does not assume triumph, but instead it involves a social critique of actions and systems that have been designed to oppress her as well as an internal recognition of her own moral weakness. In this fashion, quiet grace as the search for truth is not understood as the element that rescues black people from the bewildering pressures and perplexities of institutionalized social evils, but rather as the element that identifies possible choices of moral conduct within human interaction.

Ultimately, the search for truth and the subsequent evidence of overcoming victimization ends in self-fulfillment by rectifying one's weakness and becoming a moral agent. Cannon finds particular value in Zora Neale Hurston's fiction as a conveyor of values that the protagonist ultimately comes to embody as a means of overcoming absolute subjugation:

Hurston's characters emerge full scale with a complex and dynamic communal structure, interpreting tradition and perceptions in light of the relativity of truth, or else, their destruction becomes necessary and inevitable in the context of the community.[48]

The task of the ethicist, then, is to look at the development of African American women writers' plots to see the patterns, aims, and strategies used to overcome the dangers of living within the structures of domination. As Cannon notes in her ethical analysis of Hurston's characters, each possessed the essence of quiet grace inasmuch as "they were endowed with the ability to reduce the enigmas and elusive mysteries of social structures."[49] As women who must live in a world that is constructed to defeat them, they nevertheless refuse to be destroyed by tripartite oppression. Their ability to critically reflect on their own identity and the forces that seek to annihilate them allows them to subvert normativity.[50] The ethicist looks for evidence of black women's ingenuity in oppression, the ways in which they trump the systems that seek to dominate them.

The fifth and final step in charting quiet grace is to *critique the presuppositions, intellectual concepts, politics, and prejudice of the writer.* Many black women writers, such as Alice Walker, Toni Morrison, Gayl Jones, and Gloria Naylor are able to break out of the confines of liberal humanist tendencies and literary constraints of normative writing, creating a new language capable of articulating black women's experience from a subjective and communal standpoint. The ethicist must imagine the politics of the author embedded in the plots and portrayals of her characters. Further, the ethicist must link the author's own biography to the product of her work, not as a means of disproving what was written, but rather as a way of knowing more about the way in which her own moral maturation — garnered through her particular life experiences — informs and illuminates the indigenous wisdom of her characters.

Unshouted Courage as Theological Virtue

Unshouted courage builds upon both the self-preservation of invisible dignity and the functional prudence of quiet grace by giving spiritual value to that which is temporal. In such a way, black women can clear themselves of the contempt that permeates their identity as women in society. Thus, unshouted courage has prophetic eschatological value inasmuch as it ultimately orchestrates the prophetic implementation of divine justice. The ontology of black womanhood is exorcised from the denigrating gaze of white normativity and replaced with the redeemed value of her own culture and femininity. Herein, *love, roundness, dance, music, Moon, Spirit, Folk, Struggle, and Self* are affirmed as that which is given by God and reflects the *imago Dei* itself.

The first step in unearthing unshouted courage is to *identify "spirit helpers," indigenous people who create opportunities for transformation, who aid in shaping one's hermeneutics of suspicion.* Spirit helpers are those who nurture the black female protagonist on her journey to redemptive self-love. As Michele Jacques states in "Testimony as Embodiment: Telling the Truth and Shaming the Devil," spirit helpers are those who insist that black women

> must tell the truth about one's self and one's situation; that this truth is the way to freedom either in, through or out of the situation; that any suppression of this truth is an evil which fortifies devilish oppression; and ultimately, that this embodied testimony of truth liberates the very soul of the community.[51]

These spirit helpers provide the "a-ha" moments and oppositional lenses through which black women may redeem a sense of self-worth. As self-actualized agents who have often experienced and rallied against their own oppression, spirit helpers nurture and guide the protagonist into becoming self-actualized and critically conscious women who can confront the lies that oppress them and speak the truths that will liberate them.[52] Characters like Janie in *Their Eyes Were Watching God*, Marguerite in *I Know Why the Caged Bird Sings*, and Celie in *The Color Purple* are able to remove denigrating notions about themselves by seeing themselves not through the eyes of a racist and sexist society, but rather through the eyes of the community that loves and supports them inasmuch as they, too, are God's children. Janie offers this redeeming sense of self to Phoebe, saying: "Two things everybody's got tuh do fuh theyselves. They got tuh go tuh God, and they got tuh find out about livin' fuh theyselves."[53]

It is in this process of self-redemption that a more positive construction of self emerges. But, conversely, it is also through the process of self-redemption that a hermeneutics of suspicion is born and nurtured as a survival mechanism. The task of the ethicist is to identify those spirit helpers — literary figures such as Bertha Flowers, Janie, and Shug — who not only provide key examples for their sister characters but also protect themselves and their sisters from any threat arising from those negative images perpetuated by cultural racism and sexist exploitation.

The second step in unearthing unshouted courage and the final step in womanist virtue ethics is to *explore the revelation of God in the text*. The use of God-talk and religious symbolism is quite significant in African American women's writings for they address the way in which the mundane and the sacred are inextricably linked. The task of the ethicist is to note the transformation that occurs in the popular imagination of who God is or what God is doing in the text as the black female protagonists come into self-discovery through life's suffering within oppressive conditions. Unshouted courage is the ability of black women to see themselves as an extension of the black Christian heritage in which enslaved African Americans regarded themselves as the existing body and witness to Jesus' suffering and Christ's resurrection. Thus, as Jacques states, "the African-American Testimony is one that acknowledges inevitable victory, even in the sardonic character of life."[54]

The ethical task of mapping the testimony of redemptive self-love through God-talk is often found in the "parabolic expression" of black women's lives wherein their words, bodies, presence, and spirit reveal the very essence of God within them.[55] Just as testifying within the black church tradition reveals the presence and work of God, so too in the telling of black women's stories do they become the living expression of God's redemptive power — enabling God to speak through them as divine vessels.[56] Consequently, the result of unshouted courage is self-love because

> the womanist call to love herself "regardless" is one of the most foundationally holistic and revolutionary political actions African-American Women can take. In testifying, she puts shame to flight, the devil is defeated and the truth of Black-Women's womanists' reality of loving the Spirit, the folk, and themselves is realized in and through the roundness and fullness of their embodied presence.[57]

Diasporic Analysis

Biomythography represents the "willful behavior" of black women's enactment of radical subjectivity. Virtue ethics delineates how black women, each in their redemptive project of self-love, comes to love herself *regardless*. For its part, diasporic analysis attends to the womanist tenet of traditional communalism of black women's cultures and sensibilities. It explains the circumstances and conditions under which black women strive to foster inclusivity and freedom for the "survival and wholeness of entire people, male and female." Hence, the ethical task is to cull from black women's writings the ways in which black women work within extenuating conditions to imagine and create a space for the subversion of oppressive sociopolitical structures and for communal liberation. A diasporic analysis of black women's writings helps ethicists conceptualize the ways in which black women act as moral conveyors for their communities, those who cultivate the cultural values of the black community — "traditional universalism" and "traditional capability."

Once again, it is by looking at black women's writing that womanist ethicists examine the traditional universalism of black women's "identity" and the traditional capability of their "culture." Herein, identity and culture are linked to politicized practices rather than social location. Traditional communalism is evoked through a process wherein the collective group demystifies static notions and monolithic assumptions of black identity in order to transform their sense of who they can be while remaining black. Its identity politics is built upon an intra-communal foundation rather than one that rests upon a hegemonic referencing of what it means to be black. Traditional communalism highlights black identity and culture that is not informed by a narrow cultural nationalism which masks a continued fascination with the power of the white hegemonic other. Instead, traditional communalism, through its exploration of universality and capability of black people, refuses assimilation, imitation, or notions of black exceptionalism as viable options for those who are committed to the black liberation struggle.

Mapping Traditional Universalism

Essential to traditional communalism is the notion of traditional universality, as offered in Walker's definition: " 'Mama, why are we brown, pink, and yellow, and our cousins are white, beige, and black?' Ans.: 'Well, you know the colored race is just like a flower garden, with every color flower represented.' " The traditional universality of blackness is far more complex than what the gaze of normativity might suggest. Indeed, so much description of blackness has been from a hegemonic perspective that it is all the more necessary to invite black people to articulate for themselves what blackness is. Instead, the notion of blackness is used to give homage to the diversity, shades, and gradations of black culture rather than affix to it binary, monolithic, or essentialized cultural meanings that detract from the various realities of its peoples while furthering the legacy of colonization.

The task of mapping traditional universality is to note how black women and their communities subvert forced identities and claim an identity politics of black traditional communalism. Therefore, *blackness* is used to theorize notions of identity in a more complex, contextualized, and comprehensive way. By extension, the identity politics of black peoples across the diaspora exists as a relational as well as a provisional concern in their innumerable encounters with overwhelming whiteness and Eurocentricity. As illustrated in black women's literature, it is vitally important to recognize how black people try to find a way to survive not only within but also in spite of a dominant society and culture that is inherently predisposed to their ultimate downfall. It is in this counterhegemonic referencing that traditional communalism can be seen rather than overseen by an authoritative nation-state that claims to know black people better than black people know themselves.[58] The essential task of locating traditional universality is to render visible the ways in which black women navigate as well as negotiate a communal identity formation in the midst of particular normative notions about blackness.

Mapping Traditional Capability

The second strand of traditional communalism is about mapping traditional capability, as in " 'Mama, I'm walking to Canada and I'm taking you and a bunch of other slaves with me.' Reply: 'It wouldn't be the first time.' " Traditional capability is akin to what womanist ethicist Joan Martin calls the crux of black women's identity politics which "points toward the necessary cultural and political activity in and for African American women's moral agency — an agency that is marked by both critical deconstruction of difference as domination and the critical action of difference as creative power."[59] By extension, black women's agency is the power gleaned from the traditional universality of the black community. It mandates that black women be account-able not only to their contemporary community, which is seeking ways to attain liberation, but also that they acknowledge the constructive work of their foremothers in this selfsame task. Here again, literature is key in providing evidence of this.

The essential task of the ethicist is to show how communal iden-tity politics provokes liberative political action. Traditional capability channels the new found self-consciousness and fashions it for the purpose of collective empowerment.

Intertextuality

The ethicist's first task is to identify the intertextual presence of these two motifs, by bringing into dialogue black women's literary works from diverse geopolitical locations. Intertextuality assesses black women's literature for the ways in which blackness results in novel acts of liberation. In order to identify a universal tradition of blackness it is necessary to look at a cross section of geographies, ethnicities, or nationalities, in order to claim that blackness is rooted in a diasporic identity politics that is universal in the task of liberation.[60] Intertextual dialogue then allows the ethicist to make visible a diasporic political site — a latent and liminal space that is yet to be but always exists in the interstices, margins, and periphery of black identity — that (*a*) explores *the problem of identity* that reveals a common location in consciousness that is not geographically bound and (*b*) depicts *the novel acts* of traditional capability that evoke analogous liberatory pro-cesses undertaken by black women and their communities throughout the African Diaspora.

In studying this diasporic site, the ethicist examines the ways in which black people redefine identity away from exclusion and margin-ality as they reconnect to and remember black experiences that are otherwise dislocated by the geopolitics of nation, space, and time. The goal of this method is not merely to do a comparative analysis of vary-ing texts but rather to unearth a continuum of black moral formation across the Diaspora — through time and space — wherein we can see black women of different periods, locations, and contexts wrestling with the same issues and using similar skills to overcome them in order to mark the traditional universality and capability unique to black women. In making visible this moral continuum, the possibility of an imagined traditional community becomes a paradigm for what it means to constitute a notion of collective identity and cultural capability at the crossroads of each society's everyday material life as it is lived and transformed through individual and collective memory and re-memory, chronicled in the canon of black women's writings. Therefore, intertextual dialogue offers us a snapshot of a black diasporic political site.

Yet it is important to take into consideration not just the common experiences of oppression among black peoples but also the historically variable forms of relationality among black peoples in their various geographic formations. The ethicist must take into account how each community, and the individuals within them, are part of their own particular sociopolitical context and set of social relations (e.g., the interlocking systems of class, culture, nationality, ethnicity, gender, and sexuality). Here, it is crucial to conceptualize analytically a constantly evolving story of race from which emerges a worldwide community unified in struggle without falling into overgeneralizations that discount the diverse experiences of each black culture's realities. If we were not to take into account the diversity of black culture, we would be identifying with hegemony.

Generative Themes and Literary Illustrations

The second task that the ethicist must carry out in conducting a diasporic analysis is to note the generative themes and literary illustrations that emerge within each of the texts analyzed. Grasping traditional communalism as an imaginary diasporic political site is to understand as central the struggle of black women who have wrested their identity from the strongholds of hegemonic normativity as revealed in the lives of the protagonists. These acts and the problems they pose for black women within the Diaspora culminate in the problem of identity and the innovative acts that subvert such problems. When looking at the liberation stories of black women's communities that chart the journey from enslavement to liberation, ethicists should flesh out these two themes in their multiple and diverse manifestations. In sum, a diasporic analysis of traditional communalism must trace the survival and liberation traditions of the black community. Toward this end, the ethicist must explore the "fictions" for the purpose of making visible the ways in which these writers and their literary protagonists traditionally navigate the various politics of domination in black communal life, those of racism, sexism, and classism. In keeping with the intellectual trajectory of womanist ethics, the ethicist must particularly focus on the universal ways that black women in their diverse communities question hegemonic institutions, religious and secular. Moreover, this womanist ethical analysis also calls for identifying the canon of capabilities that black female fictional characters demonstrate as they foster both traditional communal values of survival and new critical directions for liberation.

The Problems of Identity

The investigation of traditional universality requires an in-depth analysis of the problem of identity for the black community. As represented in the question posed in the second part of Walker's definition of womanist, it is important to question the normative gaze: "If we are Black, why are we so many different colors?" Although the answer to this inquiry ("It is important for you to know that our blackness has many different shades") indicates that blackness is more than what we commonly consider it to be, it is necessary to identify, probe, and deconstruct the specific dilemmas of identity so that the diversity and universality of blackness can triumph over mainstream definitions of blackness, thus enabling black peoples across the Diaspora to envision ways to free their bodies, minds, and spirits.

In general, the problem of identity is the problem of seeing oneself and one's community through the eyes of the other. W. E. B. Du Bois identified this phenomenon of seeing and being seen as a dialectic that makes the black community self-conscious about its existence within a white supremacist hegemonic order. Du Bois states that this perennial predicament results in the very essence of the problem of identity for the black community, that of

> double-consciousness, the sense of always looking at oneself through the eyes of the other, of measuring one's soul by the tape of a world that looks on in amused contempt and pity. One ever feels [this] twoness...two souls, two thoughts, two unreconciled strivings; two warring ideals in one dark body, whose dogged strength alone keeps it from being torn asunder.[61]

At its root, the problem of identity is double-consciousness. This dialectical understanding of identity has become crystallized in such a way that it has created a fixed notion of ontological blackness, the blackness that whiteness created.[62] In shifting the ontology of blackness from one that is exclusively delimited by the dialectical (back-and-forth) entrapment of double-consciousness to one that embraces a divergent range of responses there is clearly an expansion of one's worldview. Such a broadening of one's worldview eventually constitutes traditional universality, leading from self-hatred to communal actualization. In order to give specific attention to the problem of identity, it is necessary to identify, explore, and engage the frequency in which subthemes are generated from the intertextual analysis. The generative subthemes will always involve the varied forms of internalized oppression that expose the problem of identity for the particular community under investigation.

In my own work on diasporic analysis of black women's writings, the works of African American novelist Alice Walker (*The Color Purple*), Caribbean novelist Michelle Cliff (*No Telephone from Heaven*), and South African novelist Lauretta Ncgobo (*And They Didn't Die*) are placed in intertextual dialogue with one another.[63] In each text, the problem of identity emerges within the lives of the female protagonists Celie, Clare, and Jezile and their respective communities. As each woman begins to garner clarity for herself and community by deconstructing her problem of identity, the annunciation of traditional universalism becomes the catalyst for the novel acts that result in a form of communal empowerment or liberation.

The identity narratives of the black female protagonists found in the aforementioned novels deal with becoming moral agents within an intracommunal context. In each of these novels, both the moral and identity crises of the female protagonists and their community revolve around the motif of the maternal/home — the loss of a mother, the inability to mother children, and the loss of one's motherland. Within the identity narratives of Celie, Clare, and Jezile there is a ubiquitous loss of or yearning for the maternal/home. Images of mothers and home conventionally suggest Celie's, Clare's, and Jezile's origins: birth — the start of one's being; hearth — the context of one's nurturing; and roots — the geographical and genealogical legacy that links an individual to people and places. Within each text, these female protagonists are confronted with the explicit ways in which the mother figure or notion of home has normatively been cultivated as a means of communal support and belongingness. Yet, in their own quest for traditional communalism, the deprivation of the maternal/home causes them to engender a cycle of self-hatred so profound that it renders them incapable of seeing themselves in solidarity with their communities and their communities' liberation struggles against the same tyrannical systems of oppression that subjugate them.

In all three novels, each female protagonist's self-empowerment is directly related to either her ability or inability to mother or be mothered and having a home as a context in which such a sacred process can take root. Initially what the reader bears witness to is the disruption that occurs in the identity formation of these female characters at the hands of patriarchal forces that have permeated the sacredness of the maternal home. The processes by which the female characters of these respective novels try to claim their mothering roles or actual ties with their mother is one in which the mother that they want to be is bound to redeeming their lost mothers and motherlands. Thus, the problem of identity for Celie and disruption of community begins with the impregnating rape at the hands of her father and consequential death of her mother. Literally as her mother is dying, Celie becomes a mother herself, and then that child too is taken away from her. Shortly thereafter, she is bartered off from her home and becomes surrogate mother in a home that is not hers. Her alienation from a sense of community and tradition is increased when her sister is taken away from her. However, as Celie forms community with other women who too have suffered the loss of maternal/home, collaboratively they deconstruct each other's problems of identity, resulting in novel acts of self- and communal empowerment. What Celie discovers within this sense of community is not only the diversity of black women from the southern United States to Africa but also the traditional capabilities that black women have that allow them to move beyond their individual foreboding legacies toward collective empowerment.

Like Celie's, Clare's identity narrative also begins with a young woman who suffers the loss of her mother, first by abandonment and several years later, by her death. Just as with Celie, it is Clare's loss and her yearning for both mother and home that prevent her from forming a true self. It is only when Clare returns to the island and eventually joins a militant group whose mission is to restore the traditions of her motherland, Jamaica, that she reconnects to the maternal/home. Upon accepting her call to be a mother warrior in this community, and following her grandmother's death and the realization that she herself cannot have children, Clare deconstructs in community what maternal/home is. She acquires a new home, which she literally opens up as a sanctuary in memory of her lost mother and uses it to re-create home, now conceived as a motherland free from the forces that seek their cultural destruction.

Like Celie and Clare, Jezile's identity narrative hinges on the loss of maternal/home. With every stride that Jezile makes to maintain communal traditions, she is further ostracized from it, through apartheid. First Jezile is torn from her maternal home when she marries and goes to live in the home of her mother-in-law. According to the demands of Zulu culture, she must symbolize "home" by bearing children. Yet, due to the migratory practices set up by the apartheid regime, under which rural men must seek employment within an urban setting, she is unable to be with her husband in order to conceive. Jezile's determination to visit her husband in order to fulfill the Zulu cultural expectation leads her not only to succumb to apartheid's deleterious impositions but to defy the cultural covenants made with the Zulu women of Sigageni. Further, she made a pact to refuse to accept the passes forced on them as a means of social and political control and eventually leads to her being temporarily ostracized by her community. Even when Jezile eventually becomes pregnant, she still does not assume a central place at home, since her mother-in-law assumes this position and dictates what Jezile's identity must be. Ultimately, her two children are taken away from her and she is excommunicated from her mother-in-law's home because of a pregnancy that resulted from being raped by her white employer.

In spite of these tragedies, Jezile calls upon the traditional capability she has learned from the women within her former nurturing communities. She manages to create a freer role for herself as mother and a better home for her biracial son, Lungu, the only child that she can mother. Here at her new exilic home, Jezile envisions a new maternal role and Lungu's obligation to fight for the life they wanted.

These novelists move beyond ontological blackness in order to represent traditional communalism as an identity politics that is a process of self-discovery and actualization rather than a static reified artifact. The essential attributes that come from the experiences of black people as a group, these novels show, can be used to empower that group from within. By bringing black women's writings together from across different geopolitical spaces, diasporic analysis traces the universal moral identity development of the black community and the traditional capabilities of black women in fostering communal empowerment.

Practical Strategies for Critical Engagement in Literary Analysis

Central to the task of womanist ethical literary analysis is the reader's ability to engage her literary imagination so as to immerse herself in a world of "otherness" that transcends one's own understandings and experience. Reading black women's writings for womanist ethicists allows those who do not inhabit the worlds of black women a process of world traveling. This metaphor of world traveling provides a framework in which it causes readers to question their inability to identify with black women because they are perceived as different or as an unknowable entity. Teaching black women's literature allows the reader to travel into worlds other than their own.

Black women novelists lay bare the exigencies and aspirations of their own lives and the lives of other black women. Through this inherent vulnerability, their radical subjectivity, traditional communalism, and redemptive self-love can be fully explored and differently known to strangers — thereby inviting the reader into a diasporic political site.

Yet for all this, practical strategies that facilitate world traveling are still needed. Such strategies should aid the reader in using what is chronicled and mapped to guide their incursions into the moral journey of black women's worlds.

The Dialogical Literary Journal

The following suggestions can be a helpful guide on these literary journeys:

1. Give a brief rendering of what you've read. Give your understanding of what the text *says*. Now, summarize the writing in a sentence. Then in one word: first a word from the text, then a word not in the text.

2. Identify passages in the text that captured the radical subjectivity, traditional communalism, and redemptive self-love of the characters. What did you especially like about it? Explore why and how it affected you.

3. Identify the passage in the text that you feel the author wrote in order to capture the moral significance of the novel. Include one moral learning this text brought to your understanding of racial/gender/class justice.

4. What was happening to you as you read the text? What reality inversions did you experience through the lives of these characters?

5. If you could ask the writer or any of the characters a question for your own moral development and personal growth, what would it be and who would you ask?

6. Do not claim to reside in an ethical free space/vacuum, position yourself in the text. What ideas or beliefs do you bring to the text that could influence the way you read it?

7. Choose from any of the characters in the text examples of womanist virtues: invisible dignity, quiet grace, and unshouted courage. Describe these examples, critique them, and give reasons for your judgment about the factors that shape the ethical choices elucidated by these characters.

8. What experience of your own did the text call forth? Draw out the commonalties and consequences.

9. Based on your reading, suggest a specific action you feel motivated to do in order to promote a just alternative to an unjust social trend, assumption, or practice.

10. Share this entry with another reader. Ask the reader to respond to your journal entry by answering the following questions: *What did you like about the entry? What would you like to hear more about? How does it parallel or deviate from your reading of and reflecting on the text?* Be sure to answer these same questions for your dialogue partner.

This is an exercise. Like any exercise, one mostly benefits from it by continuous and repetitive action. At the same time, this exercise mirrors the practice of literary analysis, inasmuch as identifying specific actions allows the reader to see patterns of conflicts emerging from the socially marginalized location that black women find themselves in and against which they push. In this manner, such an exercise becomes a tool that enables the reader to develop skills in detecting patterns of both real lived experiences of oppression and the worldview that emerges from them.

In addition, the exercise enables the reader to engage in a dialogical relationship with the text and context of black women's writings and lives. The reader does this not just by allowing her to enter into a worldview different from her own but also by allowing that view to inform her own moral character and process of conscientization in which the critically engaged reading of the text elicits a response from the reader. Here, a reading process that is normatively passive or monolithic becomes dialogical and diasporic. The reader comes to value that part of black women's moral wisdom in the text which she most needs in order to learn about herself in connection with otherness. It is dialogical in that, instead of keeping those worlds alien to one another, the reading process places worlds in conversation with one another.

A critically engaged reading is also diasporic because as readers engage with a variety of black women's writings, they find not only analogous patterns of oppression and resistance but also a diversity of realities that run the gamut of the African Diaspora. Thus, this exercise offers to the reader an opportunity to dialogically correlate differences between worldviews: that between reader and author, between texts from differing geopolitical realities of the black female diaspora, between literary texts and biotexts, and more.

Through this exercise, the reader can engage black women's worldview through their literature, not as mere observer and onlooker, but rather by allowing another worldview to impact her own. The reader is better able to understand the world of black women by privileging the musings and imaginations of black women as the primary lens for doing womanist ethical literary analysis. By decentering oneself, it is possible to know something or someone else; only by knowing something or someone else can one know self more fully:

> There are "worlds" we enter at our own risk, "worlds" that have agony, conquest, and arrogance as the main ingredients in their ethos. These are "worlds" that we enter out of necessity and which we would be foolish to enter playfully. But there are "worlds" that we can travel to lovingly and traveling to them is part of loving at least some of their inhabitants. The reason why I think that traveling to someone's "world" is a way of identifying with them is because by traveling to their "world" we can understand *what it is to be them and what it is to be ourselves in their eyes.* Only when we have traveled to each other's "worlds" are we fully subjects to each other.[64]

As this practical strategy shows, the reading of black women's writings becomes a call to discover worlds beyond one's own — to discover that which was once considered unnecessary — going beyond the limits of one's purview by choosing to foreground black women's worldview while placing one's own in the shadows, ultimately to make possible seeing oneself differently. The concept of world travel obliges us all to set aside our own orientations and inclinations in the hopes of critically engaging another's as a path to enhance our own perspectives and thereby facilitate radical subjectivity, traditional communalism, and redemptive self-love within the worlds of others as well as our own.

Chapter Two

A Sociology of Black Liberation as a Source for Constructive Womanist Ethics

The conventions of mainstream social scientific research frequently impose parameters of research conduct and representation of black life and culture that run counter to the motives and ethics upon black female religious life and culture.[1] As a corrective, a womanist ethical sociology of black female liberation studies black female life and culture not as a byproduct of white normative society but rather as a social system that seeks to further identify itself in light of the normative social systems that regulate its identity.[2]

Defining Womanist Sociological Analysis

A womanist sociological analysis takes seriously the task of liberation for the entire black community by examining its most subjugated class — black women. Womanist ethicists engage five tasks in articulating a black female liberation sociology: (1) examining and reintegrating black women's experience into black female society and into the wider American society; (2) debunking the social myths that denigrate black women while privileging their black male and white female counterparts; (3) constructing religious ethics and theological discourse in light of black women's experience in order to influence the approaches and sources of these fields; (4) employing a grounded theoretical approach for focusing on the hermeneutic of black female religious and cultural traditions (particularly the oral/aural cultures); and (5) envisioning an inclusive liberation perspective that seeks to dismantle the interlocking systems of oppression for all humanity, as that which is mandated by God.[3]

Womanist sociology also facilitates three dimensions of ethical analysis: First, it executes the *descriptive* task of ethical analysis by describing through empirical research the experiences of oppression that black women face. Second, it analyzes the *normative judgments* made by black women as they weigh the pros and cons of their moral situations and actions as a means for survival. Third, it facilitates the *critical/metaethical* task of answering epistemological questions by naming and defining what justice and liberation would ultimately look like in light of black women's experience of oppression and survival conditions. Inasmuch as theological ethics is grounded in the task of interpreting how people and communities make decisions based on their ultimate sacred and secular concerns, sociological methods geared toward liberation serve as an obvious tool for the purpose of womanist ethics.

The theoretical tenets of ethical analysis and the practical objectives of a sociology of black liberation together foster a womanist sociological ethic through which to interpret and transform the social world of black people. This work looks at the social world through the eyes of black women, committed to empowering them. Thus, we need quantitative and qualitative analyses of the experiences of black women and their communities, the social systems that create inequality and stratification, and the social tasks necessary for realizing black female liberation.

The Sociology of the Black Community

Sociological analyses of black women and their community have been distorted by a sociology that has focused largely on the dominant white culture to ascertain social norms and values. The black community and black women in particular have at best been measured against this alienating norm, and at worst been rendered invisible.[4] As the fields of black studies and women's studies have emerged, the experiences of black women should have been considered integral to the sociological studies of these fields. However, the normative standards of masculine blackness and white femininity have continued to exclude the salient experiences of black women's lives as relevant to these scholarly communities. Thus, when the black community is perceived as an identifiable group within society, it is defined narrowly as a race of men, just as when women are identified as a social group, those women are erroneously understood to be exclusively white. With such a normative view, as Gloria Hull et al., state, *all the women are white, and all the blacks are men!*[5]

In reaction to this one-sided approach, womanist ethicists who use sociological analysis view the primary meaning of black community as inclusive of the experiences of black women and thereby *all* black people. Inclusivity becomes imperative, not only because women make up the most marginalized and the largest part of the community, but also because they share with black men a communal identity with roots in a shared legacy of cultural racism dating from the time of enslavement and continuing to present-day discrimination.[6] Thus, the experience of the "black community" is one that is premised on a history of struggling, a legacy of surviving, and a hope of being liberated from oppression. As a social system, the black community, though diverse in its makeup and ideologies, signifies a moral imperative to advance such a trajectory. The task of a womanist sociological analysis is to adequately chart each step of this trajectory from the epistemological vantage point of black women.

Social Inequality/Social Stratification

The womanist ethical sociological perspective insists that although empirically there are numerous differences between black women, their community, and others within society, ontologically the black community is equal to all others. In keeping with its theoethical underpinnings, therefore, womanist ethicists insist that this ontological value should outweigh any empirical differences: one's humanity outweighs the particular social circumstances or characteristics that differentiate one human being from another. This liberationist and humanist trajectory is unapologetic and necessary if the social inequalities and social stratification of the black community are to be eradicated. Nonetheless, in our current social order, value is affixed to one's social circumstances rather than to one's humanity. Social stratification is institutionalized in such a way that power differentials are upheld economically and politically in perpetuity so that both present conditions and future aspirations for social mobility and future liberation are thwarted.[7] In fact, social stratification creates a permanent subhuman or second-class status for the black community and for black women in particular, so that they are forever deemed deviant. In contrast, womanist ethicists contend that it is most often the manufactured systems of social stratification and not the consequences of their empirical differences or life choices that oppress black women and their community.

The Quest for Black Liberation

The quest for black liberation requires of the scholar the ability to recall history, observe the present, and discern the expectations of black women and their communities in the midst of structural barriers grounded in cultural racism, institutionalized sexism, and capitalist exploitation.[8] The goal of black liberation necessitates both a critique of intracommunal and intercommunal systems that jeopardize the possibility of inclusivity and freedom for all, regardless or race, class, and/or gender. As a collective vision, black liberation dismisses the nihilistic and narcissistic tendencies of individualism, supporting instead a communal advancement for the purpose of transforming society at large. A womanist ethical sociological method that is committed to the task of black liberation should provide data, as Katie Cannon states, that heightens black women and their communities' sensitivity "to *what has been* in direct relationship to the viable possibilities of *what can be.*"[9] Toward this end, there are three womanist ethical sociological methods that have been developed by womanists committed to this task of liberation: (*a*) case study analysis, (*b*) the Dance of Redemption, and (*c*) emancipatory metaethnography.

) *Case Study Analysis*

Case study analysis assesses and contributes to the womanist ethical tenet of traditional communalism. Having at its core an ethic of responsibility, traditional communalism underscores both an accountability to black women's culture and health as well as a commitment to the "survival and wholeness of [an] entire people, both male *and* female." Likewise, case study analysis is intended to convey the inextricable bond between the individual found within a given case study to her larger community as well as a unique case's relevance to larger social phenomena. Serving then as living laboratory in which the researcher can gain insight into traditional tendencies, capabilities, and universality of a given group, case study analysis helps womanist ethicists inform the critical humanism that accounts for the observable behavior of black people as well as the meaning black women assign to their behavior and the secular and sacred forces that shape both their meanings and actions.

Case studies capture the critical and controversial moments and social contexts in which black women and their communities experience socioethical dilemmas. These contexts, these dilemmas, shape their engendered racial identity and moral development. In their own sociological research on religion black women ethicists use case studies as both a corrective and a learning tool for reflecting on black women and their communities' moral struggles, sentiments, and expectations. Traci West and Marcia Riggs, for example, use case studies

in their texts to address the intimate sexual violence and sexist oppression experienced by black women both in the black community
and the dominant white society.[10]

The specific case study method I use in this chapter is adopted
from Cannon's metaethical research methods.[11] I follow Cannon in
using case study methods to correct the normative traditions within
Christian social ethics research while addressing the experiences of
those who have suffered the most from oppression.

Case studies narrate real-life situations that cause us to reflect on
moral dilemmas. The researcher may use a preexisting case study or
write the case study from her own experience. Either way, the experiences and ambiguities of cases have implications for the broader
community. The goal of case study analysis is never to determine va-
lidity or prove facticity but rather to explore the moral crises that
the situation provokes due to the contestable ethical issues embedded in the case. From our womanist ethical perspective, case study
analysis calls for the researcher to be a *participant learner* who sees her
own agency implicated in the perpetuation of the moral crisis yet can
be critical in resolving the crisis through her sociological analysis of
the case study.[12] Thus, the primary objective of the researcher is to
acknowledge the moral reflexivity of her own research and identity
politics as she attempts to resolve the moral crisis of the individual
and community presented in the case study. As a *participant learner*
knowledge is constructed by using one's agency to learn from the context and one's training to work to resolve the moral crisis described
by the individuals in the case.

Finding and Recording a Case Study

A case study is a snapshot of a real-life event that captures a perennial communal concern expressed through the story of one individual's
unique moral dilemma. The story of the individual cannot and need
not reflect exactly the various forms and expressions of the particular

dilemma, but should resonate with a pervasive social concern for a particular community. At the same time, it is important for the researcher to identify stories that emerge within the black community without making predetermined assumptions and value judgments about what problems or issues ought to be described in them. Instead, it is necessary to trust that the expression of a unique moral dilemma itself reflects the crisis of a particular community at large.

Further, the case study has to be problem-based. It can take any form; it can be written as a first-person scenario or in third person; it can be a lengthy account or be as brief as a paragraph. But it must always relay a real account of a moral dilemma from which the researcher poses the metaethical inquiries of "What happened?" "How did it happen?" and "Why did it happen?" By way of illustration, I offer a retelling of a situation that was introduced in Marcia Riggs's text *Plenty Good Room* as a viable womanist metaethical case study, which I refer to as "Rev. Wanda Taylor Runs for Bishop":[13]

> *As one of the candidates for the position of Episcopal bishop, Reverend Wanda Taylor anxiously awaited the tally of the final votes and the ensuing announcement of the newly elected bishop. In the agony of the hours that passed as each district placed their vote, Rev. Taylor was wracked with hopeful despair as she considered the four decades of service she had contributed to the church that ultimately led to her designation as presiding elder and weighed it against the antagonistic reception of her among her peers and governing authority within the denomination. On the one hand, she had considered herself a prime candidate for this esteemed office because since the day she was ordained, she had worked tirelessly to fulfill this trajectory. As an ordained woman, her accomplishments surpassed those of her male contemporaries who had been promoted over her. Her record as a prime candidate for bishop spoke for itself. In her forty years of service she had: tripled memberships, increased budgets, built buildings, married and buried folk, increased the number of churches*

*in her district, served as a strong advocate for church programs, and
remained careful about her appearance and her personal life as a
woman of God, mother, and wife. On the other hand, she painfully
realized, as she overheard the scornful commentaries about her sought-
after promotion from those district delegates around her, that the
barriers to her further advancement in the church were due not to
her lack of contributions but rather to the fact that she was a part
of "a church that still does not respect woman's leadership." As she
waited for the announcement, she wavered between expectancy and
despair. In view of her merit and sacrifice, she believed she should
win the election. Yet at the same time, she also wondered why she
was continuing to value and sacrifice so much for a community that
refused to value and reward her for such sacrifices. As the tally was
read, Reverend Taylor sat in awe and disbelief that it was not her
name that was called but rather that of a man.*

Orienting Oneself to the Case Study

When the researcher brings her knowledge about the issue to the case
study, she must be willing to modify, negotiate, or sometimes set aside
completely what she "knows" for the sake of learning from the real-
lived context presented within the case. A womanist ethics stresses
that knowledge is constructed out of experience first; it is from lived
experience that theoretical inferences can be posited and tested. In
our sample case, for example, someone familiar with the ecclesial hierarchy in general or the Episcopal church in particular could make
assumptions based on their experience and knowledge about these
structures. However, such knowledge and experience cannot be ex-
trapolated to this particular denominational black church context.
More important, the situation should not be recontextualized; the parameters of the case study analysis should be limited to the contours
that the case itself sets.

Defining Contestable Ethical Issues

After reviewing the case, one defines the key ethical issues that the characters face within the case. Because the researcher may not find literal cues in the text that will explicitly name the issues that arise, her work requires the ability to draw out the underlying issues.

Contestable ethical issues are the social factors that evoke the moral dilemma for both the individual and particular community within the case study. These factors also resonate with controversial issues that we find in society at large. In order to render intelligible and take seriously the complexity of individual communities and the moral crises they face, the researcher conducting the womanist ethical case study analysis must extract, identify, and define several contestable issues, typically including issues of race, class, and gender.

The task is to define in one comprehensive sentence each contestable ethical issue found within the case study by stating *what* that issue is, *how* it is being enacted, and *why* it is upheld within the social systems that circumscribe black women and their community's livelihood. For example, in looking at the case, "Rev. Wanda Taylor Runs for Bishop," one can name gender injustice, women's leadership within the church, self-determination, double-consciousness, church hierarchies, and ministerial conduct as among the ethical issues. The researcher then defines the issues metaethically, based on the what/how/why formulation. Take gender oppression, for example: What is it? *Gender oppression* is about enforcing institutionalized discrimination against women. How is it enacted? By subordinating women to menial tasks, often referred to as women's work. Why does this happen? For the purpose of preserving male dominance within society (e.g., the church). When the what/how/why formulation is brought together, we have a complete metaethical definition of the contestable ethical issue, such as: "Gender oppression is a tool that is used to enforce institutionalized discrimination against women by subordinating them to menial tasks, often referred to as 'women's work' for the purpose of preserving male dominance within society (e.g., the church)." Such a process should be carried out for each contestable ethical issue.

Diagnosing the Metaethical Problem

The third step in womanist ethical case study analysis is to reflect on the aforementioned issues to discern and define the socioethical dilemma or metaethical problem presented in the case study. As with defining contestable ethical issues, diagnosing the metaethical problem means identifying *what* the socioethical dilemma is, *how* it is being done, and *why* it is happening. However, diagnosis of the problem must name a specific target group impacted by the socioethical dilemma in question. In normative sociological case study methods, the group or audience whom the research is about is always assumed to be the individuals named within the case. However, in womanist ethical case study analysis, this is not so. The critical distinction of this method is that it presupposes that the researcher acknowledges herself as morally committed and socially linked to the identifiable group within the case study. Such participatory learning is distinctive in highlighting the ethic of responsibility that is the mark of the traditional communalism of womanist ethical discourse. This ethic of responsibility defies the ethical vacuum and claims of objectivity pervasive within positivist social science.

Such normative research practices deny the researcher's ethical accountability for both a sound analysis and social advancement. Case in point: The late senator and celebrated Democrat Daniel Patrick Moynihan would have considered his 1965 research on single-mother families within the black community to be indicative of the pathology of the black family, inasmuch as these familial structures did not adhere to white societal norms.[14] In this manner, his own agency as a white researcher remains dominant and unreflected upon. If Moynihan had seen his own agency linked to that of the black community, it is quite likely that his thesis would not have been as death-dealing in its effect, and might instead have been empowering and life-giving to those it described. Thus, the researcher in a womanist case study analysis must socially locate herself as part of the community from which the moral dilemma emerges and is perpetuated. The gesture of stating the socioethical dilemma gleaned from the case study ("We as a...society have the tendency to...by...because...") is a just alternative for posing the problem. It makes visible the agenda and commitments of the researcher to the community.

By way of illustration, the researcher investigating the case "Rev. Wanda Taylor Runs for Bishop" would begin by assessing the definitions of the contestable ethical issues and asking herself in what ways her own social location and history might help to foster the culture and politics behind the problem in the case. Following the metaethical formula, the researcher would answer: What is the problem? *We, as clergy and church leaders, have the tendency to ignore the epidemic proportions that sexism has reached within the church.* How do we do this? *By remaining uncritical and therefore supportive of the practices of gender injustice within church hierarchies.* Why do we continue to do this? *Because we fear that if we were to identify one aspect of injustice within the church, the very foundation of our religious beliefs would collapse.*

When the what/how/why formulation is taken together, a complete metaethical statement of the problem is articulated: *We, as clergy and laity, have the tendency to ignore the epidemic proportions that sexism has reached within the church by remaining uncritical and therefore supportive of the practices of gender injustice within church hierarchies because we fear that if we were to identify one aspect of injustice within the church, the very foundation of our religious beliefs would collapse.* One can posit several moral dilemmas from this case. Essential to naming the moral dilemma is the researcher specifically articulating her context and the community (We, as _____) as a community of which she is a part which is both responsible for the perpetuation of the problem and accountable for resolving the crisis. In this particular metaethical problem, the researcher could identify with an audience (namely, church leaders and laity) that should be accountable to this particular problem and the issues that undergird it. However, a different researcher might more readily identify with the plight of Wanda Taylor. In this case, she might focus exclusively on the agency of black female church leaders, who have experienced dissonance and suffered from the discrepancies between their investments and their rewards.

The necessity of attending to the metaethical format is critical for a thoroughgoing ethical analysis because it states the thinking, doing, and being behind a problem. Often in social analysis, we are satisfied with a descriptive or empirical assessment. Or we merely pose a philosophical or psychological rendering of a problem. Womanist case study analysis distinguishes itself from other approaches by focusing on the interlocking dimensions of these categories of analysis. They allow us as researchers to examine fully the dimensions of the dilemma depicted within the case study and its complex effects on the individual's identity formation as well as on that of the community in which she finds herself. This is done in order to more succinctly address social inequality and stratification within our institutions and structures.

Citing Ethical Theory

The fourth step draws on the work of theorists who possess both scholarly and experiential epistemological privilege in connection with the communities that they study. The researcher should be attentive not only to the particularities of marginalized groups and the scholars who hold membership in them, but also to the ways in which such ethical theories clarify and enhance her theoretical orientations to studying theological ethics in general. In this manner, the scholar will see her own agency informed and shaped by the scholars trained in the field who are also members of this community. As a result, the researcher will be transformed into a participatory learner, accountable to a community that she has previously seen as separate.

The particular weakness of normative sociological method, especially in its analysis of marginalized groups, is the assumption that
the gathering of data and studying the problems that evolve from it
is in and of itself enough to reflect the value patterns, social structures, identity politics, and moral development of said group. But to
use methods without the theory that grounds or helps to interpret the
findings of research results in scholarship that lacks critical reflection
on normative institutional epistemologies. Normative epistemologies
and positivist sociology often delve into investigation on marginalized
groups in a mechanical fashion that lacks insight. In womanist case
study analysis, orienting oneself toward the theoretical implications
for using particular methods helps the researcher remove the social
sciences and institutional structures that perpetuate marginalization
and permits a resolution of the moral dilemma within the case. For
those who seek to engage in case study analysis on black women and
their communities, the contestable ethical issues at play may seem obvious. But within the issues being studied, such as gender injustice in
the case of Rev. Wanda Taylor, there may exist less obvious generative
paradigms and understandings that might modify or contradict mainstream perceptions. This is illustrated in Toinette Eugene's research
on how womanists provide alternative theories for doing research on
black women and their moral values:

> It is obvious that black women have experienced oppressive
> structures of racism, class bias, and male supremacy in both reli-
> gion and society in this country. What is not always so obvious
> to a dominant white-world view, and even to feminist theolog-
> ical understandings, is that Afro-American culture and religion
> have generated alternative interrelated notions of womanhood,
> contradictory to those of mainstream American economics, so-
> ciety, and theology. These alternative experiences, visions, and
> images of womanhood have been forged out of the furnace of a
> moral value system endemic to the Black church.[15]

Thus, in the case "Rev. Wanda Taylor Runs for Bishop," what gender injustice means for white women (and white feminist theoretical understandings) is a far cry from what it means for the protagonist, Wanda Taylor. What gender injustice means in the context of the workplace and home may be very different from what it means in the religious and spiritual life in the church. And what such injustice means in white churches is diametrically opposed to what it means in the world of the black church. As Riggs puts it, by "recognizing black women as social reformers in their own right and adding their work and insights to the base of knowledge for ethical reflection regarding black liberation,"[16] black womanist ethicists, as black women and as theorists, shed further light on the contestable ethical issues and the moral dilemmas they pose for black women.

Providing Theological Warrants and Biblical Documentation

Theological reflection that is integral to liberation is the core principle of black people's cultural tradition. Thus, God-talk and the biblical hermeneutics of black people are central to womanist theological ethics.[17] That theology emerges out of human experience is not remarkable. For black people, and black women in particular, theological reflection is often inextricably linked to identity development. As womanist theologian Jacquelyn Grant has noted, in that womanist theology understands religious ruminations and questions about God as essential to black women's experience, it is only from this perspective that an adequate ethical analysis of black women's moral and faith identity development can be done.[18]

Consider the contestable ethical issues as they emerge within Rev. Wanda Taylor's social reality. Biblical figures such as Queen Vashti and Esther or scriptural accounts from womanist biblical scholars may shed light on the issues and problems under analysis.[19] What is most important is to choose texts that resonate with the context, clarify the issues within them, and provide an eschatological vision for justice. Religious reflection plays a vital role in the perceived life chances, faith, and moral development of black women, and this step gives attention to the role that spiritual renewal and religious hope play in the lives of black people in the midst of moral crisis.

Applying Womanist Ethical Motifs

Applying a womanist ethical motif is a submethod used within womanist case study analysis. Black women ethicists' motifs attend to the two kinds of ethical judgments afforded to black women in hope of transforming their exigent moral circumstances. As Marcia Riggs states,

> On the teleological side, *racial uplift and elevation* was a matter of cultivating character traits that would contribute to the self-determination of the black community. On the deontological side, *racial obligation and duty* meant that ethical responsibility requires right acts — in this case, acts to uplift those who had less or were without educational, economic, and/or occupational advantages (my emphasis).[20]

Racial uplift addresses moral character, and racial obligation addresses moral actions. Thus, employing womanist ethical motifs in case study analysis shifts the examination from the social context to the moral character and moral agency necessary to confront such contexts. It is in this step that prescriptions and sociopolitical responses can be posited as a vehicle that can move the case toward problem solving. In considering Wanda Taylor and the community of clergy and laity, then, one must take into account the agency of all of the figures as necessary for changing the context.

The researcher may employ an individual ethical motif or several motifs to reveal directives for how to appropriately process a sociopolitical response to the moral dilemma within the case. In Riggs's own text, for example, she offers up a variety of ethical motifs that take into account the teleological and deontological sides of traditional communalism: congregational ethics, clergy/ministerial ethics, and sexual-gender ethics. Let's look in more detail at Riggs's congregational ethics motif in analyzing the "Rev. Wanda Taylor Runs for Bishop" case.

The first step in congregational ethics is to explore the moral actions of the agents within the church community for the possibility of bringing about transformation with regard to the moral life of the church. In this particular case, the researcher would want to examine the moral actions that can be undertaken to bring about gender justice.

The second step is to analyze the black church as a social institution susceptible to examination rather than revered as a sacrosanct entity beyond reproach. It is crucial that the researcher critically analyzes how the black church may be politically assertive on certain social issues (e.g., race and class) yet remain conservative, and in some cases reactionary and defensive regarding gender. To explore gender injustice, the researcher must take seriously Riggs's notion of regarding the church as a human community which must be analyzed in its various formations: the natural community, political community, community of language, community of interpretation, community of memory and understanding, and community of belief and action. This multivalent analysis allows the researcher to probe into the diversity within the traditional universality of the black community. A *natural* community addresses the physical and social needs of the members of the church community. A *political* community denotes how order is established within the church in order to execute a particular purpose or vision. A community of *language* reveals the common form of communication and rhetoric that distinguishes the church community from outsiders. A community of *interpretation* provides specific meanings of the key symbols that represent the distinct beliefs and identity of the church. A community of *memory and understanding* gives an account of the traditions that clergy and laity share. A community of *belief and action* indicates the shared commitment and professed loyalty of the church community as expressed in their actions. By examining these various modes of community, the researcher will be able to collect data that flesh out the diversity of the community while allowing for an in-depth analysis of each specific communal mode.

The third step is to explore how unequal power relationships might be reconciled. Both the ecclesial and relational practices within the church are brought into accordance with a sense of divine justice whereby men and women are perceived as equals. Here, as inspired by the seminal work of womanist sociologist Cheryl Townsend Gilkes, the interrelated structures of male-female relationships must be critically examined. The division of labor must be examined, looking at how responsibilities are divided, hierarchies are organized, and work is compensated. The hierarchical structure of power must be scrutinized to discern who controls individuals in the church and who gets controlled. Lastly, the structure of desire must be studied along gender lines to ascertain who is considered pleasing and into what roles people are placed based upon their ability to meet such expectations. Here, it is important to ask: "What does a clergyperson (or in this case a bishop) look like?" "What role does an excellent church woman have?" Again, the case per se might not seem to offer a clear in-depth answer to these questions. Nonetheless, contextual clues in the case provide enough information to allow for the poignancy of such an analysis. According to Wanda Taylor's case, the researcher can claim to know that a bishop should be male and does not necessarily have to be as sacrificial as a "good" church woman is expected to be.

In the fourth step of the congregational ethics motif, the researcher aims to expose the levels of complicity, accountability, and responsibility of the moral agents within the church as evidenced by their actions. It is important in this regard to examine whether spiritual teachings are used to mask social desires, power, and exploitation of labor. It is also necessary to illustrate the ways in which biblical interpretation and preaching prevent a thoroughgoing social analysis of the moral dilemmas and social ills perpetuated by the practices of church leaders' faith teachings. This step evaluates the church as a whole according to the moral axis of the individuals within the particular community. According to the account of Wanda Taylor, one might posit that it is due to sexism within biblical preaching and religious teachings, especially within the episcopacy, that gender injustice is perpetuated, but this is not an analysis of agency. The researcher must ask: "Who are the agents that are complicit in masking gender injustice as religious legitimation?" And "Who uses their agency to dismantle such maskings?" By implementing an ethical motif, the agents and actions of the community may be taken into account as well as the researcher's ability or inability to make a prescription (sociopolitical response) that is accountable, reflective, and responsible to the dilemma presented in the case based on such a framework.

Much like a physician, a researcher using womanist case study analysis seeks to use her training and other specialized techniques to assess the symptoms and diagnose the problems. In these five steps of womanist ethical case study analysis, a researcher may find a viable sociological analysis that empowers agents within a given community to realize the traditional capabilities and traditional universality of their agency and actions.

The Dance of Redemption

As its name implies, this womanist sociological method is devoted to the task of following the steps that one must undergo in order to realize the third womanist ethical tenet of redemptive self-love. According to Katie Cannon, who drew this method from Beverly Harrison's work on theological reflection in the struggle for women's liberation, the Dance of Redemption is an "exploratory process to discern mechanisms of exploitation and identity patterns that must be altered in order for justice to occur."[21] Within this method, womanist ethics and feminist liberationist theological ethics critically engage each other. In claiming this method, black female ethicists are appropriating the theory of white women who, conscious of their own victim/oppressor status, have dared to do what white feminism has historically failed in doing — that is, the work of analyzing the interlocking systems of tripartite oppression and the role of the self and society within it.

The Dance of Redemption has become a key paradigm within the works of womanist ethicists Katie Cannon and Marcia Riggs.[22] Womanists within theological studies and religious studies find this method essential to the task of charting the process by which black women within their communities have been able to navigate oppressive social structures and form value patterns that bring about liberation in the midst of adversity. These same womanist scholars have used this process to reflect on their adoption of a womanist orientation, name the moral conviction for doing their research, and identify the communities of women who form their research focus groups. Thus, the Dance of Redemption can be regarded as a systematic approach of liberation for a particular individual or group of women and the cultural templating of the researcher.

To initiate the analytical process of liberation, this method notes how patterns *form* values that *inform* context. For the purpose of theological ethics and womanist sensibilities, the Dance of Redemption maps the faith-moral praxis of black women who have gone through the process of redemptive self-love. Each step of this method makes evident the ways in which black women have created a notion of benevolent co-humanity as they tap into the sacred power of their own identity.

The Dance of Redemption has seven steps: conscientization, historical socioethical analysis, examining the theological resources, norm clarification, clarifying strategic options, annunciation/celebration, and re-reflection/strategic action.

Conscientization

Conscientization is that point when black women experience cognitive dissonance in light of what is considered normative in society. Whereas cognitive dissonance may be fleeting, researchers should acknowledge that conscientization is a salient experience in which black women realize that what is considered normal negates all that they embody. The initial dissonance results in a moral conviction and personal journey toward redemptive self-love that empowers one's self, community, and culture through theological reflection and social demystification.

The researcher should capture and convey the reality of conscientization as a self-revelatory process in which the researcher regards this process as a public act of denouncing social injustice on behalf of an entire community that experiences the exigencies of such alienation in various ways. The researcher should regard conscientization as the

collective "naming" process [that] fosters the ability to reflect on one's shared situation as structurally conditioned and also enables people to enter into the basic stance that precipitates ethical reflection itself: the power or capacity to be "the subjects of our lives."[23]

Historical Socioethical Analysis

Historical socioethical analysis considers the process by which black women confront the social structures and ideologies that have historically informed and maintained their oppression. In this analysis, not only does the researcher reflect upon how black women interrogate social systems of oppression, but also how they undergo self-interrogation by charting how they have been defined by and how they have come to regard as "true" the worldview that society has enforced. This process of demystifying domination, as it is considered by Cannon, makes explicit the need to mark the parameters of racism, sexism, and classism. By evaluating the social mechanisms that ascribe value to one's color, gender, and class, the historical patterns of such social mechanisms can be traced and contested.[24]

Riggs suggests that the task is to show how black women have understood their own experiences of oppression as connected to a broader historical framework. This is done by collecting actual personal narratives and connecting the patterns of oppression within them (psychological, emotional, or physical) to the ideologies that birthed them.[25] In the careful examination of the cause and ongoing dynamics of social oppression and self-subjugation, black women and the researcher may recognize that past ideologies are embedded in present realities.

Examining the Theological Resources

In the third step, the researcher charts the ways in which theological resources are used to legitimate or delegitimate the sociohistorical ideologies that have served to maintain male hierarchy, white supremacy, and economic exploitation within the church. Toward this end, the researcher examines how black women "unmask the theological rhetoric especially around issues of clericalization, that supports the complex interstructuring of patriarchal domination . . . "[26] The researcher must reflect on how theological disciplines, namely normative ethics, as well as the spiritual communities of these particular black women, have upheld or contested the structures of black women's oppression.

This type of analysis foregrounds the ways in which black women's faith praxis and liberation theology contribute to a sense of their own dignity and well-being that normative religious traditions, like Christianity, often resist. Though it flies in the face of the interpretations of many theological disciplines and faith traditions, Harrison reminds us that this personal faith/religion reflexivity should be considered neither "aberrant nor selfish."[27] Rather, in her social analysis the researcher should make evident how black women's faith evolved as these women cultivated belief systems that reflected a view of their humanity as sacred rather than spiritually bankrupt. This phase illustrates the process whereby black women attempt to liberate themselves not merely from the social stereotypes that relegate them to an inferior station within society but also from the racist and masculinist idolatry of normative religiosity that sanctions their oppression as ordained by

God. Likewise, the researcher should note what traditional tenets of black women's faith are maintained. For instance, in her study of the oral narratives of black clergywomen leaders, Africana Studies professor Deborah Austin discovers that many black women clergy have retained some of the characteristics and traditions of black church life as they simultaneously critiqued the sexist structures within them. Whether it be the celebration of either the black church confessional or conversion experience, the biblical teachings of all individuals being equal before God or the redemptive appropriation of female gender stereotypes of women as possessing the quality of nurturance, these traditions became critical theological resources for claiming personal power and spiritual ordination.[28]

Indicating the Process of Norm Clarification

The process of norm clarification is the stage at which black women's values become clearer in light of the knowledge gained from their sociohistorical analysis and theological reflection. After debunking and demystifying the structures and ideologies that seek to subjugate black women, the researcher then identifies the communities, loyalties, and solidarities that these women have formed with others who have been marginalized and oppressed.

Communities, in this regard, does not reflect those normative groups that many people deem as "community" — the family one was born into, the neighborhood within which one grew up, the church one attends, or the culture of which one is racially or ethnically a part. Instead, through the process of norm clarification, community is a politicized group wherein black women seeking liberation from oppression find others who have experienced similar alienation and who have also possibly undergone a similar conscientization process.

According to Harrison, the integrity of this type of community committed to liberation is measured by the ability of its members to stand in solidarity, holding themselves accountable to the values of the group. In that much of black women's experience in community has been characterized by betrayal, evidence of the communal context wherein black women are in relationships of *solidarity* and *accountability* with others is crucial. These two values serve as the core values of the transformative dynamic of liberation and social change.

Just as in the earlier stages of the method the researcher charted the ways in which black women deconstructed old norms, the researcher, in order to redeem a sense of self-worth and self-determination, now maps the new norms that have been constructed in an attempt to realize such aspirations. For example, Riggs's socioethical analysis on the Negro Women's Club Movement reveals that the women within this movement created a set of values that subverted the forces that kept them and their communities oppressed. In that their redemptive project of self-love was to possess and exude a politics of respectability that would liberate them from being dehumanized, the new values and norms they proposed — such as promoting and patronizing each other's businesses, possessing the spirit of independence, being economically self-determined, and acting self-assured — provided the ethical parameters through which their community would be maintained. Such self-avowed character traits, as Maria Stewart intimated in her 1832 African American Female Intelligence Society oration, are those necessary to cultivate and redeem a "character worthy of a liberated people."[29]

Clarifying Strategic Options

After clarifying communities of solidarities and the norms and values they espouse, the next area to examine is the strategic options considered and the brainstorming processes undertaken by black women in their struggle for the normative judgment and moral reasoning of black women as they make their own cost/benefit analysis. The interaction of idealistic brainstorming and consequentialist thinking is not unique to the liberation trajectory of black women. However, for a womanist liberative ethic, calculating the consequences of such strategies for black women can result in life-giving or death-dealing effects, and the line between the two is tenuous. For example, social change movements, such as the Underground Railroad and the Montgomery Improvement Association, rested not on the calculating of actions *qua* actions, but on actual lives. What Harriet Tubman and Rosa Parks accomplished as black women leaders during the Underground Railroad and civil rights movements, respectively, was not only courageous action but also calculated action that held in the balance not only their own lives, but those of countless others. Thus, the researcher should be especially attentive to how black women use their understanding of history and their place within it, the clarification of their norms and their community, as guides that ultimately lead them to consider strategic options for their own and others' liberation.

Annunciation and Celebration

Annunciation and celebration constitute the reconstructive phase in which black women integrate a sense of revivalism within the struggle of liberation. Having had to adopt the combat stance and jungle posture that is the embodiment of black women's resistance, the incorporation of communal annunciation and celebration is essential for maintaining the collective momentum and spiritual life force. Here, the womanist ethical tenet of redemptive self-love as exemplified in Walker's definition becomes embodied. The *erons*, what womanists refer to as the erotic energy that is emitted when we do the work our souls must have, and ecstasies of black women's culture are redeemed and valued as that which the struggle must have for its soul — loving the spirit, the folk, roundness, food, the moon, and herself regardless of all else. According to Harrison:

> Celebration and annunciation, then, is the phase of our theological process that enables reengagement in resistance and feeds our souls to continue the ever spiraling circle of our theological praxis, returning us to our daily engagement, grounding our power of praxis. Through it all, we discover the concrete reality

of divine and human transcendence present in radically human engagement in the question for justice.[30]

Here, the task is to note carefully how celebration is annunciated by black women within their communal context, giving special attention to those cultural features indicative of black female culture as described in the third part of Walker's definition — women embodying their unique beauty and commitment to struggle through their love of food, music, dance, spirituality, folk, and self. For example, fortified by the commitment to struggle and the promise of liberation, black social movements have often relied on the synergistic sacred and mundane aspects of black music as a vehicle for maintaining annunciation and celebration within the struggle. The spirituals of the enslaved Africans and the freedom songs of those who suffered under the wrath of Jim and Jane Crow, such as "Wade in the Water," reflect both the idealism and pragmatism necessary for black survival and liberation.

Application of Strategic Action and Re-reflection

Once the researcher has assessed how black women have integrated the saliency of conscientization, the revisionist analysis of history and theological resources, the clarification of norms and solidarities, the strategies for change, and the celebration of this process, she will also note that with a renewed sense of commitment comes a reexamination of the struggle itself and who black women and their community have become in light of the quest for liberation thus far. Thus, the strategic actions that have been reflected on further the process of a more in-depth conscientization, allowing for the redemptive project of self-love to be realized even though the struggle for liberation is not over.

The Dance of Redemption in its entirety represents a cycle that begins as an examination of self through the lens of social, political, and economic oppression and ends in an activism that seeks to change the world by annunciating and celebrating a self that is separate from that world. No longer constrained by stereotypes, myths, apostasies, alienation, or isolation, black women see themselves not as social stereotypes, but as social reformers. Black women undergoing this transformation have attained a critical reflexivity that gives them the power to change their context. Liberation is achieved along a reflection-action continuum, a process that can happen again and again.

The Dance of Redemption allows the researcher employing a womanist sociological analysis to recognize the distinction between the resilient nature of black women's identity and adaptable culture, to make visible the myths that oppressors have used to dominate society, and to explore alternatives for liberation. Implicit in this process is a teleological view of human nature that prioritizes liberation over and against the normative restrictions posed by society. Such a perspective emphasizes the role of consciousness in overcoming social obstacles. /

Emancipatory Metaethnography

Emancipatory metaethnography is another form of sociology of black liberation undergirded with womanist ethical sensibilities. This approach aims to present and embrace the experiences of black women, who are notoriously absent from discourses on faith development.[31] Womanist ethicists and theologians believe that black religious women have exhibited a profound faith — a "hope in the holler" — for divine justice in the midst of evil and suffering. The ethical insights that can be gleaned from the extraordinary testimonials of black women are valuable sources for understanding exemplary faith development. In this regard, the lives of black women can effectively serve as "organic transcripts" for ethicists and sociologists who are interested not only in studying the process of spiritual formation but have been without the adequate methods to measure such a development. Through an examination of how the lives of black women have been shaped by a sense of religious authority, scholars can map a correlation between black women's faith formation and their ability to challenge the norms and precepts of dominant society.

Emancipatory metaethnographic analysis of black women's religious formation also aims to debunk the inappropriate social scientific study of black women by treating them as subjects, not objects. This womanist sociological method is driven by an empirical research objective: to extricate the hidden value of black women's religious formation from its conventional treatment within traditional sociological analysis and religion discourse. The ethical prescription that emerges from such an objective is to carry out research in such a way that it authenticates black women's religious reflection, spiritual growth, or faith development. Toward this end, emancipatory metaethnography serves as more than a method for research: it is a transformative praxis that the womanist scholar-practitioner may use to make sacred a process that may otherwise be alienating and dehumanizing for both the researcher and the researched. This type of critical ethnography is done, as Charlene Spretnak states, so that

> we [may] value the insights that occur when women share the spiritual process that they experience, when women think about post-patriarchal spirituality and speak their truths. From these most deeply held truths grow our political convictions: "What would happen if one woman told the truth about her life? The world would split open."[32]

Thus, emancipatory metaethnography is intended to facilitate a project of recovery or discovery for scholar and subject as it seeks to overcome the ongoing tyranny over black women's faith development through normative cultural or institutional practices or through methods that render invisible the radical subjectivity of black female spirituality.

As a method in qualitative analysis, this method owes much of its orientation to the influences of *mujerista* ethics and Afrocentric sociology, especially *mujerista* ethicist Ada María Isasi-Díaz's meta-ethnographic study of Hispanic women's spirituality in *En la Lucha*. To employ this method, the researcher gives up the assumption that legitimate analysis is derived from a broad spectrum of a large sampling of women whose perspectives are reflective of a consistent pattern of thought or belief system. Instead, the researcher privileges a method that captures the in-depth perspectives of a few. Metaethnography, then, mandates that the researcher regard as valid *each* and *every* voice, regardless of how it might diverge from the others. In so doing, as Isasi-Díaz states, a metaethnographic researcher must

> believe that the voices of particular...women have validity
> in themselves and that without claiming to be representative
> they point to the reality of all...because they make our reality
> more understandable. Just as radical immanence is a different
> way of understanding what up to now has been called tran-
> scendence, so, too, the more specific and particular the voices
> we present...the more they encompass the reality of all...
> women.[33]

Convergent with the aforementioned metaethnographic approach is the practical emphasis of an Afrocentric sociology that is wedded to the task of liberative justice. Borrowing from sociologist Terry Kershaw's mandate to black studies scholars, womanist ethicists posit that one of the most significant tasks of scholar-activists is to develop research tools that help construct knowledge systems. Such an approach serves to describe, analyze, and empower black people by collaborating in changing "their dismal plights to positive prospects."[34] Like the sociological objectives of womanist case study analysis and the Dance of Redemption, the goal of emancipatory metaethnography must be linked to analysis that makes central the agency for black women to effect social change, in this case, through a sense of religious authority.

By merging the orientation of Isasi-Díaz's *mujerista* ethnography and Kershaw's Afrocentric research objectives, emancipatory meta-ethnography becomes a radicalized method for doing field research that may be used in the study of black women's theological ethics and faith development to articulate the womanist tenet of radical subjectivity. This method adds a cultural dimension that is glaringly absent in mainstream sociology and an empiricism often missing from contemporary studies of religion in general and Christian social ethics in particular.

The emancipatory metaethnographic method maps faith formation along a continuum that ranges from black women seeing themselves as the disinherited/forsaken by God to the heirs/images of God. It uses the three criteria of *cultural centrism, critical analysis,* and *spiritual empowerment* in its construction of sociology of religion to appropriately equip the researcher to map black women's faith development. Seven crucial questions provide a guide for analyzing black women's religious formation: (1) How do black women understand their world in light of their faith? (2) How do they believe their world should be? (3) What are the obstacles that have prevented their goals or dreams? (4) Were those obstacles perceived as religious manifestations and/or socially manufactured? (5) What tasks (social and spiritual) have they undertaken to eliminate those obstacles? (6) Have those tasks been successful? and (7) How do they see themselves as persons of faith in the light of such experiences?

Cultural Centrism

Emancipatory metaethnography starts with a base of black women's flesh, blood, and soul experiences. Working with the womanist theo-ethical assumption that black women are capable of making their own perspectives clear without the aid of overly processed sociological determinants or complex language and imagery, the researcher places emphasis on black women's own perspectives on their experiences, tracing the unique experiences and responses of individual black women.[35]

Scholarly training often affirms that knowledge emanates only from academic inquiry and constructed typologies. Following this logic, it would be paradoxical to believe that "subjects" could construct valid forms of knowing about themselves without scholarly articulation. An emancipatory metaethnographic method, however, transforms the re-searcher as it recognizes both the undercutting of supposed objectivity of the researcher's training and expertise as well as her dependence on the knowledge of black women — those who society in general and sociology and ethics in particular deem not only unworthy of being trusted, but also unworthy of being studied. So the real problem of so-ciology and Christian ethics is its failure to understand black women as having moral agency. Thus, cultural centrism emerges as both a critique and a correction. The scholar who grounds her work in cul-tural centrism conveys a real commitment to black women by allowing the diverse real-lived experiences and testimonies of these women to prevail as the foundation upon which knowledge will be constructed.

Simultaneously, the temporal boundaries normatively imposed by researchers give way to a research process that enables empathic comprehension and translation of black women's diverse experien-tial truths, rendering black women the authority to be the experts on their own reality, as opposed to the researcher. In *Pedagogy of the Op-pressed*, Paulo Freire calls this type of scholar a radical committed to human liberation. In Freire's view,

> [t]he more radical [she] is, the more fully [she] enters into reality so that, knowing it better, [she] can better transform it. [She] is not afraid to confront, to listen, to see the world unveiled. [She] is not afraid to meet the people or to enter into dialogue with them. [She] does not consider [herself] the proprietor of history or of [women], or the liberator of the oppressed; but [she] does commit [herself], within history to fight at their side.[36]

Cultural centrism connects with the first womanist ethical tenet of radical subjectivity. Black women's testimonials and experiences are the ground upon which any ethical analysis concerning black women's faith development must stand. By asking black women the questions — *How do you understand your world in light of your faith? How do you believe your world should be?* — the researcher taps into black women's radical subjectivity by calling into question "the radical nature of oppression and devaluation of the self... in the context of structural evil."[37] By asking the questions that are never typically asked of black women, a new threshold of knowledge is opened and an old stronghold of normative knowledge is torn down. This line of ethnographic questioning makes manifest the presence of systemic evil that is hidden and projected onto black women, due to racist projections of shame and blame found within sociological and religious discourses.

The dialogical relationship between the scholar and the group for whom liberation is sought is crucial to womanist scholars' present understanding of centrism. As it keeps the scholar attuned with how black women understand their reality separate and apart from scholarly reflections on it, this perspective better equips the researcher to translate the lived realities that inform faith development, makes visible the moral agency of black women by foregrounding diverse ways in which they reflect the image of the Divine, and helps the researcher filter through her own preconceived perspective(s) and nuances in order to remain critically reflexive.

Critical Analysis

The second methodological phase in emancipatory metaethnography is critical analysis. Having already placed black women's subjective experiences at the center of analysis through gathering testimonies, at this stage the researcher brings to bear normative and academic responses to their truth claims by asking: *What are the obstacles that have prevented their goals or dreams? Were those obstacles perceived as religious manifestations and/or socially manufactured?* In so doing, the researcher begins to implement a dialogical critical analysis that takes into account both the epistemological privilege of black women's real-lived perspectives and her own practice as a scholar. As the researcher asks black women to elaborate on the questions, she critically reflects on their responses by calling on her own training and resources to radically engage knowledge so as to dismantle the obstacles that hinder black women's self-realization.

The questions insist that both the researcher and black women wrestle with confronting the systems that subjugate black women, the normative perspectives of Eurocentric *noblesse oblige*, heteropatriarchy, and the "pedestalization" of white femininity, pushing against the systems that circumscribe not only their God-essence but their moral agency as well.

In building the various layers of knowledge — black women's testimonies, the researcher's scholarly training, as well as her grasp of society's normative perceptions of black women — we can address more completely the sometimes contradictory and always varied ways in which social forces affect the possibility for liberation. Within this context, critical analysis yields knowledge that effectively addresses the various social barriers that must be engaged and dismantled. Knowledge comes into solidarity with action. This type of critical analysis allows the scholar to escape the "circles of certainty" in positivist scholarship that insist "reality" and "truth" are predetermined and preordained. As critical ethnographer Jim Thomas states, "Critical [analytical thinkers] describe, analyze, and open to scrutiny otherwise hidden agendas, power centers, and assumptions that inhibit, repress, and constrain."[38] Therefore, a new ontological assumption (that obstacles do exist) allows us to compare the multiple perceptions of such obstacles and learn how they occur and are maintained. Critical analysis leads a critical affirmation of black women's need for alternative social and spiritual resources to aid the process of overcoming the obstacles they face.

Spiritual Empowerment

Spiritual empowerment, the last step in emancipatory metaethnography, is the process of rendering a prescriptive ethic that underscores the ways in which negative social experiences have already created or may be able to create a quickening space within which black women can actualize positive life chances. The researcher inquires: *What tasks (social and spiritual) have they undertaken to eliminate those obstacles? Have those tasks been successful? How do they see themselves as persons of faith in the light of such experiences?*

Borrowing elements from Riggs's notion of a "mediating ethic," emancipatory metaethnography is "a process of acknowledging seemingly diametrically opposing positions and creating a response that in effect interposes and communicates between the opposing sides."[39] Theory and analysis must be linked to praxis and action.

Consequently, critical analysis leads to finding a spiritual outlook that will help to transform the now perceived social consequences that black women face. The notion of God or more precisely the God within them becomes an active change agent that transforms what was once known as "natural." God as healer, provider, liberator, redeemer, and most often as the "way-maker" manifests in those actions taken up by black women who seek to solve the problems projected onto them by society. Black women's negative life experiences can be transformed not by acting within the perspectival realm of the social/objective but by seeing that their relationship with God trumps social conditions. In turn, this change is contingent on black women becoming the change that they seek. Here, the term "spiritual empowerment" describes both an activity and an ideology that is beneficial to the scholar. As spiritual activity, the term implies a call to action that may range from a modest rethinking of the role of religion in moral formation to more direct engagement that includes political activism. As an ideology, charting spiritual empowerment provides a shared body of principles about the relationship among faith, its consequences, and scholars' obligations to note the points at which immense faith trumps normative modes of reason in the extraordinary lives of marginalized people.

This step articulates the compelling ways in which women found their sense of spiritual empowerment in the midst of otherwise oppressive contexts. In this regard, spiritual awakening is that which allows the need of the Spirit to surpass the triviality and pettiness that might otherwise preclude the liberation from systems of oppression which these women so desperately seek. It is here that the experiences of black women can help researchers find the spiritual resources that allow them to move beyond socially imposed obstacles into a space where they can become self-fulfilling and self-actualizing.

As womanist scholars argue, "If the people who are the most dispossessed in our society — namely black women — are liberated and lifted up then surely everyone else will be." This methodology transforms into a humanizing vocation calling the scholar to transform her world — moving beyond the dehumanizing projections of an oppressive worldview and entering into a fuller and richer individual and collective life.[40] Authentic empowerment for change, then, is only possible when a theory of liberating ideologies is put into praxis. As Freire states, "Only in the encounter of the people with the revolutionary leaders — in their communion, in their praxis — can theory be built."[41]

Upon completion of this three-tiered strategy in tandem with the questions each step poses, researchers can successfully fulfill the womanist objective of charting radical subjectivity by relaying the narrative, generating critical authentic knowledge, and empowering black women to positively affect their life chances. To unearth these womanish ways of knowing and recognize the godliness embedded within the worldview of women of color, however, we must first fiercely and unapologetically hear their voices and see their presence, acknowledging their own agency and sense of God within a context that has long ignored their existence and insights.

Practical Strategies for Critical Engagement in Womanist Ethical Sociological Analysis

So we see that sociological analysis is a critical tool for womanist ethics in facilitating a process of reflexivity and transformation. In its critical engagement of sociological analysis, womanist ethics seeks to achieve a more authentic teaching-learning experience for the researcher, student, and research group by facilitating a social context in which scholarship and learning are freed from traditional strongholds.[42] In the traditional contexts of teaching, learning, and research, the empirical data-gathering of black women's experiences in the face of oppression could paralyze researcher and researched alike. But womanist ethical analysis, in its encounter with sociological analysis, opens up previously unseen possibilities for social transformation not only for those who we study and teach, but also for ourselves as scholars and teachers. Womanist ethical sociological analysis articulates possibilities for practitioners who seek to know in greater depth about the sociology of race, class, and gender oppression and who wish to turn this potentially volatile subject matter into reflexive, conscious ideas and practice for social change.

Womanist ethical social analysis, then, is a transformative process that requires critical self-examination by situating one's own experience and training within a framework large enough to allow black women's social empowerment to enter in. Womanists and black feminists have described this form of social analysis as a process through which those willing "to engage in the humane transformation of systems of oppression learn how these systems function. It requires an analysis of the ways in which systems of domination are erected, legitimized, reinforced, and transformed over time."[43]

Even normative approaches to Christian social ethics deem moral self-examination to be crucial. For womanist ethics, however, such a reexamination of self and one's moral character must take into account how the interconnections of race, gender, and class inform the

moral development and character formation of individuals within society. Toward this end, womanist ethicists have implemented tools in
their teaching to help students of womanist ethics critically reflect on
their own personal social formation with regards to race, ethnicity,
gender roles, and class. These tools help students lay bare the presuppositions and prejudices that must be named and deconstructed
before they attempt to analyze the lives of black women and others
different from them.

The Social Strata Inventory

The "Social Strata Inventory," as developed by Katie Cannon, is an
essential first step and practical teaching strategy for helping learners
articulate assumptions, biases, and prejudices.[44] The questions that
make up the Social Strata Inventory help students and scholars process their subjective experiences of race, class, and gender by focusing
on the first social system that people in society encounter: the family.
Though the following eight questions are geared to looking at issues
of racial and ethnic origins as a tool for critical engagement, they are
interchangeable with other social categories (such as gender, class,
sexual orientation, national identity, etc.):

1. What ethnicity and race are your grandparents? Was there a
   big difference between their cultures? Were you aware of that
   difference? What were their expectations for you based on their
   ethnic culture?

2. What were the stated and unstated assumptions about race in
   your family? How was whiteness/blackness viewed? Was it ever
   talked about? As a child, what was your understanding of race?
   Do you know what your parents' racial climate was like when
   they were children? If not, why not, and how did that shape your
   own attitude about race?

3. What is the race of the majority of your friends? How do they and their parents perceive race? How do they perceive you? Did the race of your friends change as you grew older? Did your view on race change? How and why did it change or remain the same?

4. How did your parents' ethnicity or race affect the structure of your family? Did it affect them and your family educationally, financially, or socially? If your parents were of a different race, how would your childhood have been different?

5. What has your racial climate been like? What kind of racist experiences have you personally encountered? When did you realize what your race, culture, and ethnicity meant? What do you like best about being your race? What do you hate the most about it? Why?

6. If you had an absolute choice, without any external judgment, would you change your race or ethnicity? Why and what would you want to be? When you think of blacks, whites, Latinos, Asians, Indians, and native Americans, what image do you have of them? What one word would you use to describe each group?

7. In relation to race and ethnicity, what has been your most significant gain by being who you are? The most significant loss? In what ways do social group (family, workforce, friends, religious group, etc.) reinforce racism? In what ways do they help to bring about racial justice?

8. How does answering this inventory make you feel? What have you learned? What will you now change because of it?

Womanist ethics' sociology of black liberation begins with the assumption that social oppression exists and that sociological analysis is helpful in gathering information concerning how social structures, values, and patterns within our culture make structural oppression a normative part of our society. Case study analysis, the Dance of Redemption, and emancipatory metaethnography are three examples of

sociological methods that womanist ethicists have crafted that focus
on black women's perspectives on oppression rather than society's
perspectives on black women. In so doing, the departure point for
womanist ethical sociological analysis is not deductive (having presuppositions about black women) but inductive (focusing on black
women's realities, as evidenced in the contestable ethical issues they
confront, the cognitive dissonances they experience, and the real-lived
testimonies they share). In this regard, the Social Strata Inventory is
a tool for scholar/student/practitioner to do the sort of self-cultural
templating, self-centering, and self-conscientization that is necessary
before engaging the voices and realities of black women.

The Social Strata Inventory exposes what Peter Berger refers to
as the dialectic phenomenon of social formation and human production.[45] The genealogical responses to the eight questions reveal
greater detail about how human beings create society and thereby
become products of it. Berger maintains that in the social construction of reality, humans act upon the world and the world acts back
upon humans. I draw on womanist ideology in this exercise to demonstrate that marginalization can no longer be seen as a mere external
social phenomenon, nor racism, sexism, or classism as abstract social constructs, but rather these constructs are an integral part of
an individual's most privatized cultural practice and socialization. Indeed, the history of the identity and moral formation of individuals
within their respective groups emerges as individuals are socialized to
assume and introject into their moral character, nonreflectively and
unknowingly, normative understandings of social constructs as they
hierarchically differentiate by race, class, and gender. The purpose of
womanist ethical sociological analysis, as demonstrated in this Social
Strata Inventory exercise, raises at the personal level basic questions
about structural issues of injustice and value patterns that are systematically cultivated "out there in the real world," causing the student
to reflect on the ways in which they have become integral to the
very constructs that cause and perpetuate injustice. The exercise is

useful for furthering Berger's claim by making sure the dialectical process of social construction of reality is linked to social accountability
and social justice rather than staying within a cycle of externalization,
objectification, and internalization.

Thus, the Social Strata Inventory is both an instrument for the
critical uncovering of one's complicity with social oppression and the
possible discovery of one's ability to be an agent for social change
for justice. The Social Strata Inventory helps to facilitate within the
student the cultivation of three womanist ethical tenets: radical subjectivity, traditional communalism, and redemptive self-love, not for
black women but for themselves, one's own sense of self and community large enough to begin to embrace and bring into the world
the realities and experiences different from their own and to truly engage in a reciprocal process of womanist principles: being responsible,
redemptive, communal, and engaged. In this critical engagement process, the researcher/student gets to become more than just observer
or practitioner. They become part of the womanist ethical praxis,
not only in their scholarship but in their own self-reflexivity and
socialization process.

an example in
Thomas' own
scholarship
would be
helpful-

Chapter Three

Black Women's Historiography as a Source for Constructive Womanist Ethics

i am accused of tending to the past
as if i made it
as if i sculpted it
with my own hands. i did not.
this past was waiting for me
when I came,
a monstrous unnamed baby,
and I with my mother's itch
took it to breast
and named it
History.
she is more human now,
learning languages everyday,
remembering faces, names and dates.
when she is strong enough to travel
on her own, beware, she will.

—Lucille Clifton, *I Am Accused of*
Tending to the Past, 1991

Womanist ethics would not be possible without historiography. At its core, womanist ethics engages in the practice of delineating new theories and methods of historical research that help elucidate previously unknown truths about a person, group, event, topic, or period within history. Without a firm grasp of historiography, there is nothing either particular or peculiar about the faith claims of black women. As Walker's initial definition of womanism indicates, the ingenuity and strength of black women's moral wisdom is steeped within traditions, practices, and intergenerational dialogue drawn from the shared past of black women. Thus, as Karen Baker-Fletcher states, womanist ethicists must " 'dust off' resources that have been pushed to the underside of history . . . [since] for the masses of [black] women, racism, sexism, and classism have formed the dominant context out of which their ethics of survival, resistance, and liberation have emerged."[1] Embedded within the womanist historiographical process, then, is the fundamental query: *How do you resurrect the ethical realities and concerns of black women from the "underside of history"?*

As Baker-Fletcher proposes, attending to the underside of history is a bold, audacious, and willful act. As womanist ethicists push from margin to center, the foundational truths of history as an academic discipline shift to allow room for the ethical realities of black women. As Katie Cannon implies, such work makes the womanist ethicist not only an adept scholar but a liberationist who wrests black women's ethical realities from the death-dealing grips of "false, objectified conceptualities and images that undergird the apparatuses of systemic oppression" which threaten to obliterate the truth of history and those caught within it.[2] Thus, the womanist ethical mandate is to attend to a historiography that disentangles black women's ethical realities from the pervasive as well as perpetually conjoined gazes of white supremacy and male superiority to illustrate how black women survived and subverted those gazes throughout history. It is the recovering of these stories and the moral consciousness that made them possible that drives womanist historiography. This is especially vital as it furthers the liberationist task of womanist ethicists who, prompted by Walker's definition, *want to know more and in greater depth than that which has been considered "good" and "true."*

Throughout the modern era, black people have had "proof-texts" imposed upon them.[3] In order to justify racial and gender oppression in the modern world, everything from biblical teachings to pseudo-scientific research to governmental public policy has been used to fabricate a sense of black identity and history that not only rationalized black misery in this world but also mandated that white patriarchal supremacy was God's only ordained plan for all humanity. Reclaiming the history of African Americans is not simply *revisionism,* it is actually *revivification.* For womanist ethicists, history in this case is a constant and ongoing attempt to write black women's lives, experiences, and morality back into the larger story of what it means to be human in this world so that their lives may be the indigenous sources that might rescue the oppressed from "the western metaphysic of rationalization that dispirits the world in favor of power and hierarchy."[4]

From Negro History to Black History to Womanist Historiography

The process of writing black women back into history in order to correct contemporary wrongs is indeed an effort to undo what history has done. Of course, no academic act can single-handedly erase the legacy of oppression that black women face, but intentionality makes a vital difference in the case of womanist historiography. So much of the black experience has been portrayed as a series of inevitabilities. When viewed in this way, the perennial crises facing the black community are justified by the fact that black people in this country are the descendants of African people who were ostensibly despised and reviled by Western culture. It has been nearly impossible to imagine escape from the strongholds of such disdain, let alone redeem any sense of *the good.* What does it mean to have some sense of selfhood and moral agency as a black person in America? How does one gain a positive sense of self in society while trying to wrestle with a historic context that has systematically denied black men, women, and children the basic elements of identity?

G. W. F. Hegel condemned black people as humanity in its "completely wild and untamed state" and viewed Africa as having "no historical part of the World."[5] Other so-called philosophical and pseudoscientific racist claims are found within the writings and speeches of numerous moral philosophers, scientists, and American forefathers who have been heralded throughout history as the founders of Western civilization and the epitome of American virtue. For instance, according to David Hume in his 1748 essay, "Of National Characters,"

> I am apt to suspect the Negroes . . . to be naturally inferior to the whites. There never was a civilized nation of any other complexion than white, nor even any individual eminent either in action or speculation. No ingenious manufacturers amongst them, no arts, no sciences. . . . In JAMAICA, indeed, they talk of one Negro as a man of parts and learning; but 'tis likely he is admired for very slender accomplishments, like a parrot, who speaks a few words plainly.[6]

Or in his 1764 essay *Observations on the Feeling of the Beautiful and the Sublime*, philosopher Immanuel Kant states,

> This fellow was quite black from head to foot, a clear proof that what he said was stupid.[7]

In the words of Voltaire in his "Essai sur les mouers" (1756),

> The Negro race is a species of men as different from ours. . . . They are not capable of any great application or association of ideas, and seem formed neither for the advantages nor abuses of our philosophy. They are a race peculiar to that part of Africa, the same as elephants and monkeys.[8]

As argued by Thomas Jefferson in his *Notes on the State of Virginia, Query XIV* (1787), nine years after the *Declaration of Independence,*

> Besides those of colour, figure, and hair, there are other physical distinctions proving a difference of race. They have less hair on the face and body. They secrete less by the kidneys, and more by the glands of the skin, which gives them a very strong and disagreeable odour.... It appears to me, that in memory they are equal to the whites; in reason much inferior, ... and that in imagination they are dull, tasteless, and anomalous.[9]

Although hailed in United States history as the "Great Emancipator," Abraham Lincoln asserted the following during the Fourth Debate with Stephen A. Douglas at Charleston, Illinois, September 18, 1858:

> I will say then that I am not, nor ever have been in favor of bringing about in anyway the social and political equality of the white and black races...and I will say in addition to this that there is a physical difference between the white and black races which I believe will forever forbid the two races living together on terms of social and political equality...and I as much as any other man am in favor of having the superior position assigned to the white race.[10]

In 1881, E. A. Freeman, Regius Professor of Modern History of Oxford University, exclaimed that

> America would be grand if only every Irishman would kill a Negro and be hanged for it.[11]

In the 1857 landmark United States Supreme Court decision *Dred Scott v. Sanford,* Chief Justice of the U.S. Supreme Court Roger Taney made the following declaration:

> The question is simply this: Can a negro, whose ancestors were imported into this country, and sold as slaves, become a member

of the political community formed and brought into existence by the Constitution of the Unites States, and as such become entitled to all the rights, and privileges, and immunities, guaranteed by that instrument to the citizen? . . . We think they are not, and that they are not included, and were not intended to be included, under the word "citizens" in the Constitution, and can therefore claim none of the rights and privileges which that instrument provides for and secures to citizens of the United States.[12]

Although considered a paragon of progressivism in twentieth-century America, Theodore Roosevelt made the following patently racist comments:

A perfectly stupid race can never rise to a very high plane; the Negro, for instance, has been kept down as much by lack of intellectual development as anything else.[13]

Wave upon wave of such writings had a stultifying effect on the hopes of advancing a liberationist project since they denied all but a select few people (usually kings, presidents, generals, and industrial monopolists) a guaranteed place within the historical record. In this regard, "Negro History" was needed to illustrate the simple but vital truth that black people have existed as a positive force in human affairs since the dawn of time itself. Such a recovery of history usually proceeded by looking at the race through its greatest figures. For within traditional modern historiography with its claims of being "objective," progress and achievement are measured by the presence of the "great person in history" phenomena by simply acknowledging that some special or exceptional breed of black people were present (always a small minority) at some moment in the distant past who conformed to cultural standards rather than transforming the world around them. The earliest histories written by African Americans about the experiences and accomplishments of African peoples worldwide that were produced in the late nineteenth and early twentieth centuries fell into this category of "Negro history."[14]

However, with the advent of various radical social and intellectual movements of the twentieth century — most chiefly the civil rights movement — there has been a profound paradigm shift. Previously excluded peoples of the world gained relatively more access to the studying and documenting of history. This seismic shift in the academic dimensions of history has had a palpable impact on how the larger body politic has begun to engage and relate to history. For African Americans, this transformation is best reflected in the emergence of "black history," wherein a new heterogeneous cohort of scholars built on the research of the previous generation of amateur and professional historians dealing with the African American experience.[15] In offering a critical distinction between "Negro history" and "black history," Vincent Harding contends

> While Negro History almost never questioned the basic goodness and greatness of American society, while it assumed [America's] innate potential for improvement (provided it was ready to read additional volumes on Negro History), Black History has peeped a different card. . . .
>
> Black History suggests that the American past upon which so much hope has been built never really existed and probably never will.[16]

Harding continues:

> Black History is the constant demand that the cancerous state of America be seen and known. . . . Black History cannot help but be politically oriented, for it tends toward the total redefinition of an experience which was highly political. Black History must be political, for it deals with the most political phenomenon of all — the struggle between the master and the slave,

between the colonized and colonizer, between the oppressed and the oppressor.[17]

Although the American people on the whole are less informed about history in its myriad variations, they ironically feel more entitled to lay claim to what they think is legitimately theirs whether it in fact is or not. The challenge now is not only to tell the general public about what happened in the past in accordance to the radical truth-telling provided by black history but to also inform them about why it matters. As it embraces the mandate of black history, the overarching concern in the case of womanist ethics is to challenge the apathy so often accompanied by the perennial question of "So what?"[18] According to Cannon, "We need a womanist historiography that will challenge what we presently and naively take for granted as true concerning black women."[19] In such a critique of our historical horizon, Cannon asserts that to address the "why crisis" by answering the question "So what?" ethicists become

> moral agents [who] have the responsibility to identify the so-called normative aspects of religious, social, political, cultural and economic typologies that have reproduced justifications for oppression, slavery, apartheid, and frequently genocide, invoking always a divine sanction declaring that God has ordained the natural order this way. . . . [Such] injustices . . . minimize African American women's moral agency and, in turn, make [people complicit] in reproducing conditions that thwart life.[20]

In an effort to move beyond traditionalist modes of history, it is important to recognize that people are the sum total of their history rather than history being the sum total of a people. The white patriarchal supremacy of Western culture has reinforced the logic that controlling the history of a people results in the absolute control of the people themselves. Conversely, a people in search of their own history move from being victims of circumstance to agents of change.

The cumulative experiences of black people in America are not simply a result of their origins, either cultural or natural. The appeal of history to womanist ethics is that it offers a consistent and insistent challenge to capture the rich essence of the African American experience. For instance, life stories (whether in the form of slave narratives, biographies, or autobiographies) tend to illustrate the various perspectives, issues, and events that define the lives of ordinary and illustrious individuals alike.

Embracing this historical narrative approach to womanist ethics not only demonstrates how individual lives come to represent vital generational changes, it also elevates the importance of the momentous decisions that frame moral formation within the African American community. The incorporation of history into womanist ethics illuminates how black women's ethical perspectives and concerns have been overlooked over more than half of a millennium.

The incorporation of womanist ethics into history has a humanizing effect. Interpreting history through the gaze of womanist ethics ultimately asserts black women's struggle for respect, dignity, and survival as a vital part of the human condition that can no longer be ignored. In taking up the challenge of history, womanist ethicists have written about the everyday experiences of black women for the purpose of tapping a deeply spiritual vein of wonder in the mystery of black women's history. According to Yvonne Chireau, womanist historiography attempts to bring to bear the fullness and richness of ordinary black folk in their everyday lives as a corrective.

> The introduction of the womanist paradigm to the study of religion, with its the potential for unearthing and exploring the historical, theological, social and ethical aspects of religious life, through the words, stories and acts of those who have been most marginalized, presents unique possibilities. To be sure, womanist discourse puts at its center Black-Women's sacred worlds, making the visible the invisible, speaking the unspoken through

Black-Women's actions . . . [offering] numerous prospects for the re-examination of the critical dialectic of race and gender . . . and the discourses of subjectivity in various historical contexts.[21]

Slave Narratives

The West African storytellers known as *griots* have a saying: *"However far the stream flows, it never forgets its source."* From their first arrival in the New World, people of African descent quickly became aware that without some remembrance of their history — who they were in their native land — they would most certainly be lost souls. The means of keeping those ties intact was through the oral tradition of Africa, where young people heard adults tell stories about the origins of their community and their cultural heritage. These stories were entertaining and educational. They informed the listeners of their shared past, instructed them about how to live properly, and guaranteed that this knowledge would be transmitted to future generations.

Once they were stolen from their ancestral homelands and scattered throughout the Americas, enslaved Africans continued to pass down their ancestral wisdom, morals, and values through storytelling. In turn, the tradition of storytelling became the way in which Africans best understood what was happening to them and their civilization. Under the exile of chattel slavery in the New World, the passionate need to remember traditions and family became imperative. As soon as they could, the Africans who outlived the horrors of the Middle Passage began to chronicle their stories of desperate struggle, resolve, and hard-won survival in the face of the most harrowing form of slavery in human experience. Although it was clear that passing these stories along from one generation to the next could not break the shackles of inhumane bondage or defend the weak and vulnerable from the evils of the plantation, the stories definitely nourished the souls of the enslaved, sustaining their hopes for a better world. For many generations, Africans in America cultivated a thriving appreciation for history *qua* collective memory through oral storytelling. It was the only means they had to communicate their pains, hopes, fears, and desires. Even as some limited — in many cases, stolen — opportunities arose for black men and women to disseminate their histories more widely using print media, the dominant genre and vehicle for relating their stories was the slave narrative.

Numerous scholars of great renown and stature have sought to examine the literature of slave narratives in order to grasp some understanding of the collective experience of antebellum African Americans who had escaped and found their way to safety in the North.[22] Often, rather than investigating the personal experiences of enslaved black histories to better understand black resiliency and resistance in the face of formidable oppression, these scholars have examined these narratives in terms of the white imaginations of biblical allusions, the rhetoric of abolitionism, and the stirring autobiographies of black histories that fit into northern white liberal sensibilities and their religious and social movements. Because slave narratives were collected and recorded for this essential reason, these narratives were considered valid only when prefaced by letters of authenticity from a white abolitionist. Thus, slave narratives were written first and foremost in order to appeal to white audiences — "appeal" being a concept that can be construed both narrowly and broadly. Often the texts of the narrative were edited by a white hand to portray African Americans as pathetic and lamentable creatures — as victims rather than as American heroes and heroines with privileged epistemologies.

Slave narratives were not regarded as the moral wisdom of people who had fled and survived the most horrific form of human savagery, nor were they understood as lenses to gaze into the sociopathic and heathenistic minds of a white slavocracy. Rather, they were written to amass compelling evidence against the political bulwark, economic mainstay, and religious orthodoxy of southern slavery and to secure the political hegemony, industrial capitalism, and religious heterodoxy of northern paternalism. Thus, both northern abolitionism (pity of black histories) and southern slavocracy (contempt of black histories) objectified black people and their histories, leaving black people forever enslaved to the controlling interests and imaginations of whiteness.[23] Drawing principally from Black women's slave narratives, womanist ethicists investigate this paramount ethical query: at what point and under what conditions did enslaved women of African descent in America reclaim their status as members of the moral universe?

Slave Narratives as the Roots of Radical Subjectivity
in Womanist Historiography

Womanist ethicists have been unapologetic students of slave narratives. Embedded within these narratives lie not only the stories of individual black women and their people's strivings for freedom from oppression, but also the horrific truth concerning the social manufacturing and religious roots of racism, sexism, and classism as American core values. During the period of chattel slavery, religion and oppression based on race, gender, and class combined to sustain the worst form of abuse ever known to humankind.

No other institution or ideology has made the dehumanization, brutality, and terrorism of black people in general, and black women in particular, a religious mandate and social pastime. America's Christian slavocracy, with compulsory labor as its right arm and sexual victimization as its left, shackled black women as it tore them away from their homes and families, and ultimately tried to destroy them using the full arm of the law, demands of the marketplace, and racist teachings of the Bible. Thus, without the perversely legitimizing and entertaining value that black women's subjugation provided for the general American public, the United States would not be the burgeoning world power it is today. It is a historical fact that truths are inscribed upon the bodies and in the memories of black women. Slave narratives provide a profound insight into the radical subjectivity within black women's history.

Radical subjectivity, as the first womanist ethical tenet, is clearly represented by black women's slave narratives. These testimonials of black women's experiences from slavery to freedom, either written or dictated, have had a profound impact on the chronicling of the black experience. According to historian V. P. Franklin,

> the slave narratives laid the foundation not only for the African-American autobiographical tradition, but also for novels and short fiction produced by black writers in the nineteenth century. There was a close resemblance in structure and organization between the slave narratives and the early novels. . . . The heroes or heroines were introduced, subjected to certain types of cruelty and oppression that were inherent in their condition, fled the oppressive circumstances, and subsequently became involved in larger movements to end the injustice and oppression.[24]

In this fashion, slave narratives advanced a vision of radical subjectivity as a core element of the African American literary, intellectual, and theological traditions. Moreover, this connection between slave narratives and the larger canon of African American cultural and intellectual production is effectively driven by the ethical mandate that, once liberated from ignorance and oppression, each person should do likewise for others. Beyond an individual testament of one black person's struggle to overcome and escape the "peculiar institution," slave narratives are also a critical ethical discourse between the oppressed (in this instance, the enslaved) and the oppressor (the entire slaveholding class) in American society. Slave narratives represent a bold moral intervention by the disinherited, dispossessed, and disenfranchised to reclaim both their humanity and their history. As womanist ethicist Joan Martin asserts in her examination of the slave narrative of Bethany Veney ("Aunt Betty") written in 1889, "Aunt Betty understood that by writing her own story, she was writing *into* history the story of millions of women, men, and children whose multigenerational struggle was slipping from the nation's memory as if it never occurred."[25]

Situating the slave narratives of enslaved black women within the historiographical context of womanist ethics is important for three reasons. First, these statements of faith and experience are crucial documents that chronicle the worldview of people who actually endured enslavement and inhumane abuse. The very existence of these slave narratives flies directly in the face of any conviction by mainstream society that America has always treated the rights and liberties of its citizens with fairness and dignity. To read and incorporate even one of these women's slave narratives into the broad sweep of U.S. history is to reveal to be a sham the dominant cultural mythology of America as the land of liberty.

Second, the lives and perspectives of these women need to be recognized and redeemed as inspirations for contemporary generations. Under the triple yoke of racial, gender, and class oppression, enslaved women were denied by the harshest law and social custom the opportunity to learn how to read or write. This made the creation of the slave narratives a rebellious act, especially as it was undertaken by black women. In telling the truths about their lives in the midst of slavery, these women were engaged in a sort of "outlaw discourse," challenging the politics of exclusion. As bell hooks notes, the immense power of black women's slave narratives as outlaw discourse hinges on the fact that they "emerge from a practical engagement with cultural practices and cultural icons who are defined as on the edge, as pushing the limits, disturbing the conventional, acceptable politics of representation."[26] Thus, the ethical function of black women's slave narratives is indeed radical subjectivity as outlaw discourse. By declaring the dehumanizing atrocities that were enacted against them and denouncing their abusers, black women who survived enslavement radically transformed the possibility for moral critique in this society.

Third, the function of the slave narrative was a liberating praxis in and of itself for black women who were never supposed to attain literacy. As Joan Martin contends, "enslaved women's narratives *set free* the lives of women who were propertied objects and artifacts of others' history; the narratives made them the subjects of history."[27]

Herein lies the key concern of radical subjectivity as a facet of womanist ethics. Even within the confines of a society that sought to render these women's pains invisible to the normative gaze of history, a representative group of enslaved women spoke out, often at great personal jeopardy, about their rightful (as well as righteous) discontent with their predicaments in this country.[28] Regardless of the risk to life and limb, however, the slave narratives of black women had a sacred, transcendent quality, attesting to their own self-definitions and their religious viewpoints.

A recurring theme in the slave narratives is an assertion of how these enslaved women understood that their resistance and survival were contingent on their actions as guided by their personal relationship with God. As an outgrowth of Christian testimony, black women's slave narratives reveal an intimate relationship with the divine expressed in song, prayer, preaching, and the prophetic revelation that the goodness of God is defined in freedom for all. As black liberation theologian James Cone would argue, the slave narratives demonstrate dialectical relation within these testimonies wherein "the story was both the medium through which the truth was communicated and also a constituent of truth itself. In the telling of a truthful story, the reality of liberation to which the story pointed was also revealed in the actual *telling* of the story itself."[29]

Black women whose lives and confessions formed the basis of the slave narratives provide a deep historical grounding for womanist theologians and ethicists because enslaved women held fast to the concept of a God that promised freedom, not slavery, as a key article of their faith. In their embrace of a multidimensional approach that grapples with theological, ethical, sociocultural, and economic aspects of black women's historical experiences of oppression via the slave narratives, womanist scholars such as Katie Cannon, Jacquelyn Grant, Delores Williams, Joan Martin, and others examine these rich resources for contemporary understandings of black women's roles, contributions, and critiques within church and society.

Though the slave narrative was a product of enslaved black men and women who were fugitives, the record and publishing of these narratives were forced to attend to a specific pattern necessary to appeal to the humanitarian aspirations, social ideals, and Christian sympathies of the imagined white audience. According to James Olney's anatomy of slave narratives, the standard historiographical readings of slave narratives had to satisfy twelve elements in order to pass the litmus test of authenticity.[30] Thus the teleology of the slave narrative was its suitability and believability as a story that white readers wished to hear. Consequently, for much of the twentieth century, historians, sociologists, and anthropologists have wrestled with or overlooked the need to articulate the vision of emancipation chronicled in the black experience of enslavement. Thus, theological ethical discourse has largely missed truly profound liberation theologies and liberationist ethics *rooted in* the memories, testaments, and histories of black women's struggle in and freedom from slavery.[31]

In contrast to normative treatments of slave narratives, womanist ethicists have engaged in ongoing efforts to generate new formats and methods that help to make available the moral wisdom and unknown truths of these texts to future generations of Americans. They are looking to glean the "outrageous, audacious, courageous and willful behavior" that led enslaved black women to freedom. Through exploring the classic slave narrative canon of the 1700s and 1800s, the Work Progress Administration transcripts, and the "neo-slave narratives" of contemporary African American female literati, a new narrative ethic charting the radical subjectivity of enslaved black women can be revealed.[32]

According to his assessment of the narrative and life of Frederick Douglass, ethicist Scott Williamson asserts that the two most
crucial insights of a narrative approach to reading slave narratives
are that (1) moral character and social circumstance co-evolve, and
(2) although individuals' inherit moral system(s) from their community and context, individuals weed out some of what they inherit.
According to Williamson's narrative approach, enslaved black histories simultaneously shaped and were shaped by the moral discourse of
their day.[33]

Using the tenet of radical subjectivity, a womanist narrative method
for analyzing black women's slave narratives produces quite different
and more poignant observations than those of Williamson. First, the
moral character of bondwomen defied their social circumstance. To
be sure, the institution of slavery affected black women's conditions.
But social conditions and moral character are not simply a by-product
of one's social condition. Such an assumption dismisses the power
dynamics between slaveholder and enslaved while it also diminishes
the role of self-empowerment in facing hierarchical power. The classic
narratives of Harriet Jacobs and Sojourner Truth attest to the bond-
woman's ability to maintain — or even attain — a sense of dignity
and self-worth that is in contradistinction to her social station. As
black women's historian Deborah Gray White makes clear, the shift
of historiography to focus on the brutality of enslaved black women
and their moral resistance to it shows us a different interpretation of
these women:

> African and African-American women were not born degraded
> but rendered so by enslavement. Were I to write *Ar'n't I a
> Woman?* today, I would use the verb "enslaved" rather than
> the noun "slave" to implicate the inhumane actions of white
> people. The noun "slave" suggests a state of mind and being
> that is absolute and unmediated by an enslaver. "Enslaved" says
> more about what happened to black people without unwittingly

discriminating the sum total of who they were. "Enslaved" forces us to remember that black men and women were Africans and African-Americans before they were forced into slavery and had a new — and denigrating — identity assigned to them.[34]

If moral character and social circumstances co-evolved, as Williamson contends, to be sure these women were indeed "slaves" and not "enslaved."

Second, the moral system(s) of these enslaved black women formed, informed, and transformed not only their moral systems and those of others around them, but often altered their social circumstances as well. The moral acts of black women were more than a give-and-take or push-and-pull with the powers that be. Rather, the small and larger acts of resistance waged by bondwomen were nothing less than a war fought against the powerful elite white slaveholders who sought to defy their moral existence. Thus, as historian Stephanie Camp claims in her study of the everyday resistance of enslaved women, the study of resistance to slavery must change in light of this resilience, for it was those womanish acts (whether visible or invisible, shouted or unshouted) that opened toward freedom:[35]

Enslaved people's many forms of resistance were struggles for life without reference to their owners as well as responses to their owners' efforts to deny them, for instance, access to their families or time alone. It is planters who attest to how much slaves' search for space and time to themselves mattered *in their own time*; slaveholders' violent actions and their words illustrate the extent to which some slave activities cut them to the quick by challenging their authority and, they feared, by making their plantations less efficient. That enslaved people were willing to risk gruesome punishments for the sake of a degree of mobility speaks volumes about its importance to them.[36]

Such radical subjectivity provides an appropriate lens for understanding the unique formation of enslaved black women's moral character and moral systems. Differing from Olney's anatomy or Williamson's narrative approach, a womanist narrative ethic measures the process by which these women fearlessly sought to articulate their own moral framework without need of white affirmation or fear of white retribution. The researcher may mark this ethical process by attending to four critical junctures within the slave narrative: moral crisis, spiritual confession, escape from slavery, and speaking truth to power.

Moral Crisis

The actual capture and enslavement process often marks the moral crisis of the enslaved African. As demonstrated in Harriet Jacobs's slave narrative, "I was born a slave" is a statement of fact that generally denotes an ethical observation of his/her social condition. As such, *being born into* slavery does not necessarily capture the sense of crisis in being *captured and stolen into* slavery. Since most of the slave narratives of black women were stories of being born into slavery, a different point of existential angst and unresolved tension within the narrative must serve as the entry point for charting the radical subjectivity of these women. The point of moral crisis is the event or circumstance that provokes the enslaved black woman to rescue herself from an impending disaster so great that it threatens her more than the institution of slavery itself. This moral crisis is a circumstance womanists refer to often as "death-dealing" or, as historian Nell Irvin Painter has diagnosed in her studies on black women's enslavement, "soul murder."

According to Painter, soul murder is the point at which the hallmarks of oppression (like slavery, patriarchy, free-market capitalism, and Constantinian Christianity[37]) and their death-dealing vestiges of serial rape, depraved indifference, mental torment, and physical torture unite to create a sense of trauma so great that it seeks to sever enslaved women from their "world of feeling" and their moral sensibilities. Soul murder attempts to make them obedient and submissive vessels in an effort to "make hallmarks of oppression as both one's social reference and moral center."[38] Using insights gathered from psychiatric studies of child abuse and research on the horrors of the Vietnam War, Painter likens slave narratives to trauma literature.[39] Traumatized people — such as abused children, war victims, and enslaved women — threaten to submerge themselves, suppress their emotions, and surrender to the machinations of their abusers.[40]

Yet within the slave narratives of black women, there is an instant where such impending annihilation is eluded. The researcher should look for these contestable moments where, in the face of great adversity, commingled with pain, anger, rage, and fear, these women garner moral strength and clarity to set out on a journey for freedom. We see this clearly in the narrative of Harriet Jacobs. After being threatened, beaten, and accosted numerous times by her lecherous enslaver, Mr. Flint, Harriet (referred to as Linda Brent in her narrative) was given one final and last ultimatum to succumb to his desires to be his concubine or face dire circumstances. As the narrative indicates, Flint states:

> " . . . my interest in you is unchanged . . . you desire freedom for yourself and your children, and you can obtain it only through me. . . . You know I exact obedience from my own children, and I consider you as yet a child. . . . You accept my offer?"
>
> "No, sir," [Harriet firmly responds.]
>
> His anger was ready to break loose. . . . On what a monstrous chance hung the destiny of my children! . . . I foresaw the position I should occupy in his establishment. I had once been sent to the plantation for punishment. . . . My mind was made up; I was resolved that I would foil my master and save my children, or I would perish in that attempt. . . . I had a woman's pride, and a mother's love for my children; and I resolved that out of the

darkness of this hour a brighter dawn should rise for them. My master had power and law on his side; I had a determined will.[41]

"A woman's pride," "mother's love," and "determined will" are analogous to the womanist ethical tenet of radical subjectivity, a subjectivity that saved Harriet from the grips of certain death. Thus, by concentrating on the moral crisis embedded within slave narratives, not only can we "learn a great deal about what they were likely to feel, or want to do, or try to get away from," as Painter states, but more important we can garner a sense of "how" and "why" they sought to confront, survive, and overcome slavery.[42]

Spiritual Confession

Seeking spiritual welfare in the midst of social warfare, enslaved women and men articulated an explicit moral and religious framework that served as their ethical guide. According to literary scholar Melvin Dixon:

> This was no mystical yearning, but a real test of character and conviction. As realists, [enslaved women and men] demanded that they be struck dead to sin in order to live again in freedom. In order for this transformation to be real enough to connect with the vital image of deliverance, "conversion had to be in the nature of a stroke of lightning which would enter at the top of their head and emerge from their toes." Slaves, as Paul Radin continues, "had to meet God, be baptized by him in the river of Jordan, personally, and become identified with him."[43]

This moment of spiritual sanctification and moral transformation becomes the pivotal point wherein radical subjectivity is not only a political act but also a divinely inspired one. The narrative of Sojourner Truth (born Isabella Baumfree) poignantly illustrates this. As many historians who retell Truth's narrative are aware, Truth's life story was not written by her (she was illiterate) but retold and recorded by a white governess, Olive Gilbert. Isabella Baumfree had determined herself to be free of the economic, psychological, and sexual exploitation of her former owner John Dumont, but she was about to entertain his advances. Yet, as Gilbert recounts from Truth's narrative, before she was about to succumb to his devices,

> God revealed himself to her, with all the suddenness of a flash of lightning, showing her, "in the twinkling of an eye, that he was *all over*" — that he pervaded the universe — "and that there was no place where God was not." She became instantly conscious of her great sin in forgetting her almighty Friend and "ever-present help in time of trouble." All here unfilled promises arose before her, like a vexed sea whose waves run mountain high; and her soul, which seemed but one mass of lies, shrunk back aghast from the "awful look" of Him whom she had formerly talked to, as if he had been a being like herself; and she would now fain have hid herself in the bowels of the earth, to have escaped his dread presence.[44]

In a recent documentary entitled "There Is a River," historian Margaret Washington depicts this moment of profound spiritual transformation as

> a mighty fire that's burning all around her but instead of it being flame, it's wind. And it consumes her. And she doesn't know how long she's in this state, this very fearful, very frightening state. But when she comes to herself, she's standing out there in the yard, and all she can say is, "God! I didn't know you were so big!" . . . It's at this point that she becomes aware of, in her mind, the fact that Jesus is the intermediary that will always protect her; and that to her is a spiritual conversion. It is baptism for her.[45]

This confession of spiritual transformation is not a single moment in black women's slave narratives, but often the confession becomes a refrain that rekindles the sense of an omnipresent, omniscient, and omnipotent God who works intimately with the oppressed. Sixteen years after her first conversion experience of baptism by lightning, fire, and wind, Isabella Baumfree has another talk with Jesus that concretizes her spiritual rebirth.

> When I left the house of bondage, I left everything behind. I went to the Lord and asked Him to give me a new name. And the Lord gave me Sojourner, because I was to travel up and down the land, showin' the people their sins, an bein' a sign unto them. I told the Lord I wanted another name and the Lord gave me Truth, because I was to declare the truth to the people.[46]

Spiritual confession serves as a second phase for charting radical subjectivity within a womanist historiographical framework. This testimonial mode of the slave narrative rejects a notion of Christianity that had once enslaved them and creates one that inclines itself to a higher standard, a morality and spiritual discourse with an all-powerful, knowing, and present God. As womanist historian Rachel Harding states, women like Sojourner Truth "did not assume the Christianity of their oppressors. The Christianity that [they] assumed was a Christianity that they created . . . [one] that they reevaluated and reconfigured to fit their needs."[47]

Escape from Slavery

The escape from slavery marks the climax of the standard reading of slave narratives. Normative historical analyses of "the escape from slavery" highlight cloaked descriptions of failed attempts to flee the pursuit of bounty hunters and their dogs or "successful attempt(s) to escape, lying by during the day, traveling by night guided by the North Star, reception in a free state by Quakers who offer a lavish breakfast and much genial thee/thou conversation."[48] But womanist ethicists chart escape from mental and spiritual enslavement as well. These enslavements are not escaped if one flees one white home in exchange for another. Rather, freedom existed in a subjective sense for these women and countless others like them wherein it could not be given or taken by whites but had to be felt by and known for themselves. According to Emilie Townes, a constant mainstay for enslaved black women's radical subjectivity "was that women were able to interact with one another." Known as "doctor women" who brought into life the wanted or terminated the unwanted babies of enslaved women, or "other-mothers" who took care of children not born of their womb, or "gang leaders," who meted out their own measure of authority in subversive ways, or "forewomen," who had charge of the female and children sector of the plantation, or "conjure women" who created potions and roots that provided healing, comfort, and vindication — even in the midst of enslavement, these "certain women" worked to be freeing agents in the lives of their enslaved sister-folk.[49] Although enslaved, they were black women who continuously sought to mete out moments of freedom and frequently "disrupted plantation life," Townes says in her reflections of Deborah Gray White's classic text *Ar'n't I a Woman?* Whether it's "prophetess Sinda who was able to stop work on Butler Island in Georgia with her prediction that the world would come to an end on a certain day" or "Big Lucy [who] had more control over [her enslaver's] female slaves than he did," these women held the key to the small and large manifestations of freedom.[50] And it was because of this radical subjectivity that "slaveowners were least likely to separate mothers and daughters."[51]

Through such an analytical lens, the researcher can see that Harriet Jacobs's experiences of freedom from slavery were only successful because of the collaborative efforts of other enslaved women as well as her daughter Ellen. Freedom, as Harriet Jacobs's journey attests, consists of a series of radical subjective acts made by one woman in order to incite radical subjectivity in another woman. Foreshadowing the courageous yet necessary radical acts that would need to be enacted by later women, Harriet's grandmother set forth the standard of radical subjectivity in her rebuke of Mr. Flint's sexual advances and attempts to sequester Harriet from her home. Harriet's grandmother freed her grandchild, if only for a moment, when she exclaimed,

> "Get out of my house!...Go home, and take care of your wife and children, and you will have enough to do, without watching my family....I tell you what, Dr. Flint," said she, "you ain't got many more years to live and you'd better be saying your prayers. It will take 'em all, and more too, to wash the dirt off your soul...." He left the house in a great rage.[52]

The rebellious act launched Harriet into preparations for her escape — an escape that relied on the collaboration through communication, silence, and courage of one enslaved woman to conceal another. Betty, a cook who was a stranger to Harriet, conceals Harriet in her mistress's house. Betty's first words to Harriet have the ring of a solemn vow: "Honey you is safe. Dem devils ain't coming to search *dis* house."[53] While she tended to Harriet's physical safety, Betty, with a local network of other enslaved women, also attended to her psychological state as she kept her updated on the status of her children. Under Betty's close watch, Harriet found her longest hiding place and refuge in a shed concealed in plain view of her children with whom she could not communicate lest she threaten their freedom. Determined to be free for herself but also *for* her children and *with* her children, Harriet recounts:

> My friends feared I should become a cripple for life; and I was so weary of my long imprisonment that, had it not been for the hope of serving my children, I should have been thankful to die; but, for their sakes, I was willing to bear on....[54] I hardly expect that the reader will credit me, when I affirm that I lived in that little dismal hole, almost deprived of light and air, and with no space to move my limbs, for nearly seven years.[55]

Even Ellen, Harriet's young daughter, played a courageous role in aiding her and her mother's journey to freedom. Unbeknownst to many who assumed that Harriet had escaped north to freedom, Ellen, who had been made aware of her mother's seclusion, carried with her "the weighty secret that weighed down her young heart" even when she was taken to New York with another family.[56] And ultimately, Harriet's intercession on behalf of her poor friend Fanny who, unknowingly, was "many weeks hidden within call" of her again illustrates the risks that one enslaved woman would take for another.[57] Though fatigued, crippled, and willing to forsake her own escape, Harriet successfully lifted another into freedom.[58] Like Harriet Tubman's series of radical acts that nurtured as much as it forced others into freedom, Jacobs's narrative depicts a figurative underground railroad of courageous women who knew that freedom was just a sister away.

Speaking Truth to Power

Regarded as property, and having no ownership of themselves, enslaved were not only forbidden to read or write but were oftentimes beaten and punished for any form of verbal assertion. Thus, communication and self-expression were sacred acts for enslaved people, especially women whose every word was guarded in the houses, fields, and beds of their slavemasters. It is no wonder, as Yuval Taylor states, that "self-expression, then, was one of the greatest boons of freedom — witness the joy of Harriet Jacobs's exclamation, 'What a comfort it is, to be free to *say* so!' "[59] The mere act of speaking, writing, and expressing lies behind the black church proclamation, "Let the redeemed of the Lord say so!"

The *telos* of the slave narrative, the final act of radical subjectivity, is the moral resistance formed by enslaved black women in order to speak truth to power. Placing the truth at the center, the scholar of womanist ethics may unearth moral treasures in these historical testaments that function to document a subjective account of the horrific conditions of slavery, convince the reader of the evils of white supremacy, impart a liberating theology in the midst of theodicy, validate the moral character and personhood of black women, redeem what it means to be black, female, and free, and, ultimately, to write into history a story of enslavement and escape that might rescue others from such fate. This may be evident in the case of Sojourner Truth, who

> traveled thousands of miles speaking about her extraordinary life, women's rights, and the evils of slavery. Her anti-slavery speeches placed her at the center of the most volatile civil debate that the nation would ever know. She joined those of her generation who forged the issue of slavery into a moral argument that tore the country in two.[60]

Sojourner Truth's words are a prime example of the act of speaking truth to power. The voice of Sojourner Truth served abolitionist and suffragist history as a clarion call for the truth to be proclaimed everywhere injustice was observed, and passed on to generations who lack the resources for discerning it. Having overcome crises, encountered the awesomeness of God, and escaped to freedom, just what compels these women to boldly speak truth to power? Why risk such vulnerability and possible retribution? In her study on Sojourner Truth's life and meaning, Painter notes that Truth had observed the plight of black histories in the North as a

> "great drama" no more than "one great system of robbery and wrong..." The material hardship that she was witnessing, and that she felt she was contributing to, intensified her holiness convictions. Thus, she deeply believed she was called by the Spirit to live up to her name which not only meant what she had earlier proclaimed it to be nor solely the appropriation of the title "of her erstwhile spiritual leader, the Prophet Matthias, who had called himself the 'Spirit of Truth.'" But rather she became the vessel of God's rebuke and liberation: "sent by God the Father and Jesus the Son... to convince people of sin and judgment" (John 16:7–16)[61] as well as the one upon whom the "Spirit of

the Lord" had come and anointed her "to preach the gospel to the poor . . . to heal the brokenhearted, to preach deliverance to the captives, and recovering of sight to the blind, to set at liberty them that are bruised. To preach the acceptable year of the Lord" (Luke 4:18–19).

According to Painter, speaking truth to power had been long in the making for Truth, whose wrestling with truth-telling started when she was just a girl. Her long-standing struggle for voicing the truth was transformed into a vocation as she took on a name "that designated her role as preacher."[62]

Whether as preoccupation, vocation, or occupation, the task of speaking truth to power was the work of justice and advocacy for others who lacked the ability or opportunity to express the injustices they encountered. So radical is this speaking out that it renders freedom itself as ambiguous. As Jacobs recalls, hers is a story that seemingly "ends with freedom; not in the usual way" but rather as one institution giving way to another. Whether reconciling one's own freedom in the face of those who still find it a far-off reality or still wanting something more than the presumed definition of freedom, these women no longer perceived freedom as a final destination designated by others but as a transcendent space one forever strives to attain, not merely for herself but for everyone else. This was the freedom for a place Harriet Jacobs yearned for, as a radical place "where the wicked would cease from troubling, and the weary are at rest."[63]

Moral Biography/Autobiographical Method

Following in the footsteps of the slave narratives both literally and figuratively, moral biography and autobiography provide invaluable and important resources for womanist ethicists. These sources can reveal much about the historical exigencies and ethical framework that gave rise to life in the contemporary black community. Rooted within moral biography and autobiography are the acts of "witnessing" and "testifying," which are related to the second womanist ethical tenet of traditional communalism. As womanist ethicist Rosetta Ross illustrates, "witnessing" and "testifying" within black religious vernacular culture has come to represent the "ritualized mundane" wherein everyday life is made sacred by the willful assertion of divine intervention in ordinary circumstances. According to Ross, "Rooted in accounts of slaves and ex-slaves after conversion experiences, testimonies in African-American religion are verbal affirmations of belief and narratives of divine interaction with ordinary life."[64] Although the nomenclature, context, and circumstances for black people's production changed with emancipation, the impetus remained consistent over generations. Within the black community, the desire to live our lives and tell our truths is wonderfully captured in the phraseology of "witnessing and testifying." Taken in tandem, these terms are far more than simply black religious idioms. These concepts are the very wellspring of constructive ethics and liberationist praxis within the overall scope of the black religious experience. Ross defines the terms in the following manner:

> [T]*estifying* occurs both as [an] interpersonal narration of divine interaction with everyday life and as a formal portion of worship wherein believers share in community what God has done in their lives.... Testimonies require the presence of witnesses, persons who also have seen or experienced God's work and who are able to certify or attest to the truth of it in the testimonies they hear. By identifying oneself as a witness, a believer asserts that she has personally experienced God's provision or other intervention. Moreover...the term *witnessing* has arisen as a complementary way of naming the believer's ordinary moral practice — way of living — as religious practice.[65]

As Ross suggests, witnessing and testifying are a prime formulation of a dialectical process whereby black people recount stories of their personal knowledge of God and individual experiences of divine mercy but also recount daily existences worthy of an outpouring of God's grace. Bound together in this way, witnessing and testifying are the resonant and reflexive hub of African American moral development.

As African Americans attempted to define a social reality beyond the yoke of slavery, the initiation of a full-fledged biographical and autobiographical tradition became an indispensable means for reconstructing the historical meaning of blackness in modern society. Emilie Townes rightfully notes that

> biography and autobiography can provide the critical tools for a fuller recovery of history. These genres/disciplines enable the researcher to expand his or her vision of society in a historical epoch. He or she can concentrate on individuals or events. In using biography, the researcher is provided with one type of lens to enter a culture if not a society. Autobiography provides a similar lens. Both genres must be used carefully to expand the worldview of the subject and to place that worldview in its cultural and social context.[66]

How are these disparate stories of individual black lives woven together into a larger historical fabric that represents the concerns of the race? Africana studies scholar and literary critic Henry Louis Gates Jr. notes that

> for hundreds of black authors, the most important written statement they could make seems to have been the publication of their life stories. Through autobiography, these writers could, at once, shape a public "self" in language, and protest the degradation of their ethnic group by the multiple forms of American racism. The ultimate form of protest...was to register in print the existence of a "black self" that had transcended the limitations and restrictions that racism had placed on the personal development of the black individual.[67]

This "impulse of autobiography," in Gates's terms, has an implicitly political, ideological, and moral core. According to Gates, having been

> deprived of access to literacy, the tools of citizenship, denied the rights of selfhood by law, philosophy, and pseudo-science, and denied as well the possibility ... of possessing a collective history as a people, black Americans — commencing with the slave narratives in 1760 — published their *individual* histories in astonishing numbers, in a larger attempt to narrate the collective history of "the race." If the individual black self could not exist before the law, it could, and would, be of the black self and against the social and political evils that delimited individual and group equality for all African Americans.[68]

Not only does Gates deem this autobiographical tradition (and its biographical counterpart) as one directly descended from the genre of slave narratives, he also views it as a radically redemptive historical project in which black people — individually and collectively — can reassert themselves in the dominant transcript of the human past.

It is important here to recall that the black community is not by any means a monolithic whole, but rather a complex entity awaiting deeper analysis. The richness and dynamism of black people's engagement with their places in history as well as their regard for divinity offer a wealth of theo-ethical resources. In his assessment of the significance and diversity of perspectives within black theological discourse, Christian social ethicist Robert Michael Franklin contends that

> much of it does not adequately attend to the host of issues related to personal identity, wholeness, and fulfillment. ... These traditions have paid insufficient attention to the manner in which people ought to be transformed and equipped to live in the new society that is thought to be emerging. This general inattention to the personal dimension of the liberation enterprise has important consequences. Failure to understand the person-centered

dimension of a broader, inclusive societal transformation can lead to a disturbing paradox: an optimism concerning the future of society existing alongside personal and familial disintegration, despair, and frustration.[69]

To resolve this critical imbalance within black theology and ethics, Franklin asserts that it is necessary "to identify the finest and most-trusted resources and reflections on personal wholeness in the modern black community and to present them for revision, reconsideration, and possible reappropriation. The time has come for a hermeneutics of recovery."[70] This notion is further advanced by Emilie Townes, who asserts that

> biography has a two-fold purpose: the recovery of the individual or institution, and the illumination of the era in which that person or institution is representative. The subject must be recovered in such a way that it does not become larger than the times of which it is a member. Neither the subject nor the era can be explored with great integrity without a constant dialogue between the two. Both function to shape each other.[71]

For womanist ethics the use of biography and autobiography must be invested with a hermeneutics of recovery but also a keen sense of historicity. In revealing the importance of achieving such a balanced perspective, Townes's insights are particularly helpful. For Townes,

> the "truth" must be told with integrity in using biography as a method for Black historical recovery. This entails an intentional method of uncovering as much of the remnants of the historical epoch as possible. The researcher must take care to uncover the individual's reflections as well as the reflections of those around him or her. It is poor scholarship to use the biographical method to create larger than life (and inaccurate and untruthful) figures no matter how racist or oppressive history has been as a discipline. Little is served in "creating" an historical figure.[72]

To defend against conservative denouncements of revisionist historical research, the truth gleaned from a biography or autobiography must be portrayed without embellishment or invective. The process of historical recovery using biographies and autobiographies as moral resources is intended for the *rescue* of "lost" wisdom and unheard voices of African Americans (whether past or present) and not as some measure of *revenge* against the discipline of history itself.

Townes indicates several key elements of black autobiography: "political awareness, empathy for suffering, the ability to break down the dualism of 'I' and 'You,' knowledge of oppression and the discovery of coping mechanisms, shared triumph, and communal responsibility."[73] As important as these concepts are for womanist ethics, they do not adequately capture the motive force within this cultural tradition, namely that the story being told is a direct extension of the life being lived. In a great majority of black women's biographies and autobiographies, their lives, activities, and worldviews are a continuation of those practices and principles they gained in community; in a sense, this harkens back to the West African adage "I am because we are." In much the same manner as the "spiritual autobiographies" in the Western canon dating from *The Confessions of St. Augustine* in the fifth century to the present day, the black woman's moral biography/autobiography is often a bona fide testament of her faith, validating her personal dignity as well as attesting to the value of the black community, and affirming the acceptance of living a changed life.

In the spirit of "conversion rhetoric" prevalent within the black Christian experience, the question has never been *why* tell the story of "how I got over" but, more importantly, *how.* In her deconstruction of testifying and witnessing within the black community, Rosetta Ross asserts that

testimony occurs because one, in the vernacular of the tradition, "has to tell somebody." The speech about what God has done arises from the power of an encounter with God that makes it impossible "to keep it to myself." Subsequent to the encounter motivating testimony as speech is the expectation of living in ways that reflect having had the encounter — adjusting or changing one's behavior.... The assertion of having an encounter with God — generally understood as an internal personal experience — coincides with the Christian conception of God's spirit being active within a person.[74]

In other words, telling the truth about one's life is one thing, and living a life worthy of such revelation is something altogether different. The struggle for womanist ethics is to reconcile these two realities in a way to inform contemporary and future generations.

So also according to literary critic Hazel Carby,

[Black women] cannot hope to reconstitute ourselves in all our absences, or to rectify the ill-conceived presences that invade herstory from history, but we do wish to bear witness to our own herstories.... What we will do is to offer ways in which the "triple" oppression of gender, race, and class can be understood, in its specificity, and also as it determines the lives of black women.[75]

Cultivating and Using a Hermeneutic of Recovery

In the first step of moral biographical/autobiographical method the researcher uncovers and identifies the story and truths of a historical black woman's life. Here, the researcher finds black women's truths and questions whether black women really have a truth or story worth telling.

Charting the Genealogy of Knowledge

The second step, charting the genealogy of knowledge, should unpack and examine the line of dissent, especially its theoethical predecessors and political resources, while paying attention to "web of mutuality" in which black women are interwoven.[76] Their ideals for communal survival and black empowerment were part of a legacy bigger and more encompassing than a particular moment in time. Like the "fictive kin" and "extended family," social mainstays of the black community tradition, black women had ideological forebears, spiritual helpers, and other-mothers whose visions and philosophies helped to shape their own.

Observation of the Reverent Disclosure

The observation of the reverent disclosure is the third step in the moral biographical/autobiographical method. Here I am indebted to the work of Rosetta Ross. This step takes into account that within most of black intellectual production (slave narratives to current-day black and womanist theological discourse) when black people give themselves over to a thing and try to account for why they do it, their stories take on a confessional posture. It is no coincidence that the *Confessions of St. Augustine,* regarded as the first spiritual auto-biography, was written by a man from North Africa. At some point in their stories, black women talk about how they came to know God (or Truth) for themselves — how they discerned what was morally good or right. This notion of coming to know God may be passed down from mother to daughter or sister to sister (i.e., Ella Baker and Sep-tima Clark), or it may come as Sojourner Truth's "touch from God" or Rosa Parks's inspiration from the story (or spirit) of Emmett Till.

It is for the researcher to reckon with how the presence of God, spirituality, or other-worldliness affected the world of the mundane — accepting that divine intervention can intercede in the mundane, that the sacred may be observed operating in human affairs.

Reconciliation of the Unfinished Life

The final step in moral biographical/autobiographical method is the reconciliation of the unfinished life. In this stage, the researcher must synthesize what has been recovered, known, and disclosed as pulling together the common threads that make up the fabric of the particular black woman's life. Most biographies and autobiographies have only one certain ending: "and she died." In the spirit of traditional communalism, however, the black community looks for legacy and longevity beyond the grave, hoping to draw connections to issues or events beyond a single life. When we speak of our dead, they live as ancestors in our memory and re-memory. By uttering their memory, we conjure their essence back into being. Their stories stitch them into history and stitch our lives into their legacy.

The life and legacy of Rosa Parks is prime for the application of this method. Arguably the best available account of Rosa Parks's life is offered in her memoir, *Rosa Parks: My Story.* Here, Parks narrates her autobiography over the course of many hours of interviewing by Jim Haskins, her ghostwriter who also is author of notable biographies of former Congresswoman Barbara Jordan and musical composer Scott Joplin. The collaborative effort by these two native Alabamans produced an autobiography expressly aimed at younger readers with two explicit purposes: to convey her view on her commitment to Christian faith in a world of evil and hatred fueled by the racist perversion of Christianity by white supremacists such as the KKK; and to share with a new generation the generally ignored aspects of her life's work in the black freedom struggle. Amidst the many sources to consult concerning her life, the first step in cultivating a hermeneutic of recovery would clearly be to seek out her autobiography as the primary source for this method.

Applying the autobiographical method's second step — charting the genealogy of knowledge — allows us to examine the lines of dissent throughout Parks's life. At this stage of the process, researchers must approach historical documents with strict attention to mapping the ways in which people, events, and issues converge in order to demonstrate what we "know" about the past. By gleaning aspects of Parks's life and constructing a narrative around her experiences we develop a deeper understanding of her role in making history.

Although Rosa Parks became enshrined in world history as the "mother of the civil rights movement," she was born Rosa Louise McCauley in Tuskegee, Alabama, on February 4, 1913. Her parents, James and Leona McCauley, separated when she was still a young child, and she moved with her mother to Montgomery. There she grew up in an extended family that included her maternal grandparents and her younger brother, Sylvester. As both anecdotal and historical evidence support, Montgomery was hardly a hospitable city for African Americans in the early half of the twentieth century. As she grew up, Rosa was forced into segregated all-black schools, such as the Montgomery Industrial School for Girls. After the Montgomery Industrial School for Girls had been targeted by the Ku Klux Klan and eventually closed, she was unable to continue her studies because she had to care for her ailing grandmother and mother by the time she was sixteen. As she got older, she went on to Alabama State Teachers' College for Negroes but her education was disrupted by a number of family crises. Moreover, she faced daily rounds of racist laws and social customs governing her behavior in public places.

At twenty years old, Rosa McCauley married Raymond Parks. The couple both held jobs in the local community — Raymond as a barber and Rosa as a seamstress — and they enjoyed a modest degree of comfort and prosperity. Eventually, with the support of her husband, Rosa Parks was able to devote time to her formal education and earned her high school diploma in 1934. As a couple, Rosa and Raymond Parks were very involved in civil rights activism in Montgomery during the 1930s. In addition to their efforts to help free the "Scottsboro Boys," the infamous case in Alabama where nine African American men were falsely accused of raping two white women, the couple became active members of the NAACP, and Mrs. Parks served as secretary and eventually youth leader of the Montgomery chapter. In addition, she became a very active member in the Montgomery Voters League, a group that helped African Americans to pass a special poll test so they could register to vote. Their conscious commitment to racial equality was woven deeply into the fabric of the couple's marriage.

Like many other black southerners of her generation, Rosa Parks was no stranger to white intimidation. For instance, she often boycotted the public facilities marked "Colored," walking up stairs rather than taking elevators. She had a special distaste for the city's public transportation, as did many of her fellow black citizens. The Jim Crow rules for the public bus system in Montgomery almost defy belief today. Black customers had to enter the bus at the front door, pay the fare, exit the front door and climb aboard again at the rear door. Even though the majority of bus passengers were black, the front four rows of seats were always reserved for white customers. As historian Robin Kelley argues, public transportation in Alabama was alternately a *congested* and *contested* terrain in which African American resistance to white supremacy was routinely exercised during the apex of Jim and Jane Crow.[77] In fact, Parks herself was once thrown off a bus for refusing to endure the charade of entry by the back door. In the year preceding Parks's fateful bus ride three other African American women had been arrested for refusing to give their seats to white men. In spite of this, the system remained firmly entrenched and, as a result, Mrs. Parks often preferred to walk home to avoid the humiliation of the bus.

Tracking reverent disclosure in Parks's life — the third step — brings us to these reflections on her religious upbringing. Rosa Parks states, "I have been a member of the African Methodist Episcopal (A.M.E.) church all of my life," writes Parks. "My father's brother-in-law was pastor of the [Mount Zion] A.M.E. Church in Pine Level, Alabama. The denomination became known as 'The Freedom Church' during the abolitionist movement. It was the spiritual home of many well-known black persons in our history before civil rights. They include Bishop Richard Allen (the founder of the A.M.E. Church), Frederick Douglass, Harriet Tubman, Sojourner Truth, and others.

They all were strongly rooted in the A.M.E. church."[78] The observation of reverent disclosure requires a sharp focus on how religious faith informed the lives and actions of historic figures by means of surveying documentary evidence for such links and references.

Parks was also committed to the theological vision and cultural heritage of the church. Years after the civil rights movement had become a part of history, she discussed the church's role in the black freedom struggle. Parks recalled that "people often ask me, 'Why was the church a part of the movement?'... The church was and is the foundation of our community. It became our strength, our refuge, and our haven. We would pray, sing, and meet in church. We would use Scriptures, testimonies, and hymns to strengthen us against all the hatred and violence going on around us."[79] "My strength has always come from the church. I have always gained strength from thinking about the Bible and from the faith of my family. Church has always been a place where we can turn to God for rest and encouragement. It lifts the spirit and helps us to go on."[80]

In addition to her early life experience, Rosa Parks's fortuitous opportunity to attend the Highlander Folk School helped profoundly shape her personal and spiritual outlook about activism and social justice. At a crucial stage of her life, Parks received a two-week scholarship to attend workshop sessions in Monteagle, Tennessee, on various civil rights issues such as school desegregation and voting rights. It was an idyllic setting with an atmosphere of interracial camaraderie. Even in the omnipresent threat of Klan violence and general outrage by local whites, Parks's time at Highlander offered her a vision that other noteworthy leaders of the civil rights movement such as James Bevel, Marion Barry Jr., Julian Bond, Diane Nash, John Lewis, and Martin Luther King Jr. created on their treks to the Highlander Folk School during the 1950s. Each of them, including Parks, received invaluable skills and training as well as reassurance that they were not alone in the often difficult, thankless work of social justice. This latter issue was especially true for Rosa Parks who, during her brief stint at the school, met black women such as Septima Clark, who would serve as a lifelong role model. In her encounter with Clark, she found an example of black womanhood who was strong, determined, compassionate, and vivacious — traits that would carry her through the desperate struggles that were to come. Although this event was short-lived, Parks glimpsed the full potential of traditional communalism at work in the world around her. In the final step of the moral biographical/autobiographical method, the researcher synthesizes what has been recovered, known, and disclosed about a particular black woman's life such as Rosa Parks.

On December 1, 1955, Rosa Parks had a particularly exhausting day. She was employed as a seamstress at the Montgomery Fair department store, and she had spent the day pressing numerous pairs of pants. She has since admitted that her back and shoulders ached terribly that day — she was forty-two at the time — and she deliberately let one full bus pass in order to find a seat on the next one. The seat she eventually found was in the middle section of the bus, because the back was filled. A few stops further down the line, a white man got on and demanded a seat. The driver ordered Parks and three other black customers to move. The other riders did as they were told, but Parks quietly refused to give up her place. When the driver threatened to call the police, Parks said, "Go ahead and call them."

Parks was subsequently driven to the police station, booked, fingerprinted, and jailed that same evening. Parks was granted one telephone call, and she used it to contact E. D. Nixon. As a black labor leader, prominent member of the local NAACP branch, and a leading figure in the Montgomery Improvement Association (MIA), Nixon was one of the foremost civil rights activists in the state. Upon hearing of Parks's ordeal, Nixon was properly outraged, but he also sensed that in Parks, his community might have the perfect individual to serve as a symbol of enduring injustice in the South. Nixon called a liberal white lawyer, Clifford Durr, who agreed to represent Parks. The fact that Rosa Parks had worked for Clifford and Virginia

Durr, a couple who had committed themselves to liberal causes in the pursuit of social justice, was nothing short of providence. After consulting with the attorney, her husband, and her mother, Rosa Parks agreed to undertake a court challenge of the segregationist law that had led to her arrest. The profound sense of community of the support and counsel that Parks received from friends, family, and colleagues allowed Parks to make this pivotal decision that eventually transformed American society.

Word of the arrest spread quickly through Montgomery's black community, and several influential black leaders decided the time was ripe to try a boycott of the public transportation system. One of these leaders, Jo Ann Robinson, used the mimeograph machine at the nearby college to make several thousand copies of a leaflet advertising the boycott. The message of the leaflet was plain: "Don't ride the bus to work, to town, to school, or any place Monday, December 5. . . . If you work, take a cab, or share a ride, or walk." The boycott of Montgomery's city buses by African Americans was virtually universal on December 5, 1955. A meeting on the subject that evening drew an overflow crowd numbering in the thousands, and a decision was made to continue the boycott indefinitely. On Tuesday, December 6, Parks was found guilty of failure to comply with a city ordinance and fined $14. She and her attorney appealed the ruling while the boycott lasted for a total of 381 days. When the U.S. Supreme Court deemed segregation of public transportation unconstitutional, the Montgomery bus boycott officially ended on December 21, 1956. With this legal proclamation by the high court, Rosa Parks's simple yet bold gesture was transformed into a legendary mode of silent, dignified protest that would form the basis of the black freedom struggle in the United States.

One of the main concerns of womanist historiography is to deconstruct the prevalent myth that Rosa Parks was just a good-hearted, middle-aged seamstress who was simply too tired from working all day

to give up her seat. Arduous work and decisions groomed Parks politically and empowered her not only to say "no" on December 1, 1955,
but also gave way for her individual refusal to become the basis for
a full-blown constitutional assault on Montgomery's bus segregation
ordinance. For example, Rosa Parks's biographer, Douglas Brinkley,
writes, "While the NAACP executives made dinner speeches and
attended national conferences," it was Parks, as the local NAACP
secretary, who

> balanced the ledgers, kept the books, and recorded every report
> of racial discrimination that crossed her desk. She also did field
> research, traveling from towns like Union Springs to cities like
> Selma to interview African Americans with legal complaints, in-
> cluding some who had witnessed the murders of blacks by whites
> in rural areas.[81]

At the very least, a sustained look at the life and times of Rosa
Parks illustrates that the defense of liberty and human dignity was not
easy. Parks and her family received numerous death threats and almost
constant telephone harassment by the angry white populace of Montgomery and elsewhere. The strain actually caused Raymond Parks to
suffer a nervous breakdown. In 1957, Rosa and Raymond Parks and
her mother relocated north to Detroit, Michigan. The move was also
motivated by the jealousy that reared its ugly head among the male
chauvinist black clergy and the emerging civil rights leadership. Black
men, especially black preachers, were not used to sharing the spotlight
with women. Envy was especially evident with male colleagues like
E. D. Nixon and the Rev. Ralph Abernathy, who began making Rosa's
life miserable by belittling her and her husband. And it was not only
the men. Female plaintiffs in a concurrent antisegregation lawsuit were
"angry that everybody was saying 'Rosa this' and 'Rosa that.' They
felt they deserved the public adulation, the NAACP-sponsored trips
to New York, the invitations to speak, and the praise from Dr. King
as much as she did."[82]

If Rosa Parks was safer in Detroit, she was never quite allowed to recede into anonymity. Over the next few years, she was sought out repeatedly as a dignified spokesperson for the civil rights movement and received honorary degrees by a number of universities. Following both the March on Washington and the assassination of President John F. Kennedy, she decided to become deeply involved in local politics in Detroit. By 1964, Parks had volunteered to work on the congressional campaign of a then-unknown black civil rights lawyer named John Conyers. Once he won the seat in the House of Representatives, she eventually obtained a long-standing and prestigious job on his staff for more than twenty years. Although she retired in 1988, her advanced age did not rob Rosa Parks of her quiet beauty, pride, and grace, nor did it restrict her travels and activities. She still made some twenty-five to thirty personal appearances per year and was a vocal opponent of apartheid in South Africa. Her crowning achievement, however, is the Rosa and Raymond Parks Institute for Self Development, which she founded in Detroit. The institute offers career training for teenagers with special attention to education and motivation.

Through the institute, Parks oversaw programs such as "Pathways to Freedom," which encourages young people to learn about their heritage and reach their potential. Meanwhile, she received numerous awards, including the prestigious Medal of Freedom award from President Bill Clinton in 1996, the first International Freedom Conductor Award given by the National Underground Railroad Freedom Center in 1988, the Detroit-Windsor International Freedom Festival Freedom Award, and the Congressional Gold Medal of Honor in 1999.

The culmination of this type of analysis is the reconciliation of the unreconciled life. However, this is more than a rote summary or conclusion. In the final stage of this process, the reconciliation of the unfinished life by researchers is an effort to reassess the overall integrity of one's life in light of the revelations provided by the preceding stages. Reconciling the elements of Rosa Parks's unfinished life, for instance, means seeing life and activism as being defined by more than her well-known act of heroism.

Until her death in October 2005, more than half a century after making her decision to continue sitting on a segregated Montgomery, Alabama, bus, Parks was a living legend. Her legacy is felt every day by Americans of all backgrounds, races, and creeds. But in becoming an icon, Parks also had been turned into a shadow of her real self. Few people are aware of her lifetime of struggle before and after that fateful day in December 1955 or of her low-key but indispensable work to build the NAACP. There is a general failure to recognize that Parks held her own political views. There is much to learn from the incredible story of Rosa Parks, as a woman, not an icon. The mission of womanist historiography is to ensure that such vital life stories are never reduced to a single isolated moment.

Ella Baker's life presents a contrasting example, especially in regards to the hermeneutic of recovery. Although Ella Baker was known and revered by a generation of grassroots civil rights organizers and activists nationwide, her name is virtually unrecognized by many people today. Yet she persisted as a black woman in national organizations, working as an organizer/educator for five decades. Most people familiar with Baker's role in the civil rights movement recognize her as a founding mentor of the Student Nonviolent Coordinating Committee (SNCC) who taught the oppressed rural poor how to resist oppression, challenge entrenched power, and speak truth to the grievous conditions of their lives. Baker insisted that leadership for the black community must emerge from the courage, experiences, suffering, and understanding of ordinary, often illiterate, people in the Mississippi Delta. Demonstrated by her brave work in Lowndes County, Alabama, and in Albany, Georgia, Baker trained students who, in turn, initiated the Freedom Rides, the voter registration drives, and Mississippi Summer. Baker taught these young activists to learn from — and be transformed by — older, more experienced grassroots leaders as well as to respect their wisdom in a dynamic, group-centered manner. Neither fixed nor finished, she remained a work in progress. In this fashion, she encouraged a spirit of radical, democratic humanism that influenced the black freedom movement, labor, the women's movement, the student antiwar movement, GIs and veterans, prison and solidarity work, and community organizing for decades to come.

In charting the genealogy of knowledge in Baker's life, we find that she was first and foremost a youth organizer. After arriving in Harlem in 1927, she helped to found her first youth organization in 1930. The Young Negroes' Cooperative League (YNCL) membership consisted of black youth, from their teen years to their mid-thirties, committed to consumer education and small-scale cooperative ventures like buying clubs, grocery stores, and bulk distribution networks. Once elected national director by her peers, Baker pursued economic power through cooperative Harlem ventures. She believed that cooperatives emphasized the values of interdependency, group decision-making, and shared economic resources that enable a community to master its own destiny.

Most of all, Baker sought to increase the social, political, and economic understanding of black youth in the 1930s. By using an informal informative approach to African American youth, she aimed to educate and lead her peers into self-directed action. The current generation of youth organizers now tout consumer education, financial literacy, credit unions, and cooperatives as viable strategies for confronting persistent urban poverty and the obscene inequities of globalization, but it was Ella Baker's pioneering efforts that made such concepts both feasible and fundamental. Her sense of traditional communalism was inextricably linked to the prospects of making racial uplift a practical reality.

Throughout the 1930s, Ella Baker expanded her commitment to the principles of local youth organizing, primarily in Harlem. She chaired the Youth Committee of One Hundred, worked with the Young People's Community Forum, and served as an advisor to the

New York NAACP Youth Council. In 1938, Baker applied for the national NAACP position of youth director. Although she did not get the position, the outgoing acting youth director asked her to apply again two years later. Despite her impressive roster of recommendations that included A. Philip Randolph and the Urban League's Lester Granger, Baker was once again denied the national directorship of the NAACP Youth Councils. In 1941, she joined the staff of the NAACP as assistant field secretary. She would later become director of branches, establishing a vast network of grassroots contacts in African American communities throughout the South. It was this network of relationships built in the 1940s that formed the foundation for much of the civil rights activity of the 1950s and 1960s.

Although in charge of the development of adult chapters, Baker encouraged and kept in touch with the youth councils. The NAACP never trusted or allowed Ella Baker to fully develop the potential of the Youth Councils in the 1940s; they feared independent, organized black youth, as established civil rights organizations still do today. Despite the NAACP's attempt to prevent Baker from formally organizing black youth, her web of contacts in the South proved an indispensable resource when she returned to working with young volunteers in 1960 and created the SNCC.

Above all, Ella Baker was the connecting force that brought young people together with their radical elders, northerners with southerners, fundraising with community organizing, leadership training with collaborative modes of teamwork with intellectuals and ordinary people. In a spirit of true innovation and dedication to the black community, she developed a network of organizational and personal relationships out of which emerged an independent youth organization that represented a true alternative to the more politically moderate civil rights organizations of her time. Since Baker's death, no leader has emerged who is committed to strengthening the ties that bind fragmented social and political action to the twin goals of spiritual enlightenment and human empowerment. Ella Baker tilled the soil of social change

no one leader
but several leaders

for at least two decades in preparation for the 1960s student movement. It took patience, vision, humility, and faith. Regretfully, current
generations of youth have not found their Ella Baker.

Regarding the observation of reverent disclosure in Baker's life,
Barbara Ransby notes:

> During her childhood in Littleton [North Carolina], Ella Baker
> was nurtured, educated, and challenged by a community of
> strong, hard-working, deeply religious black people — most of
> them women — who celebrated their accomplishments and
> recognized their class advantage, but who also pledged them-
> selves to serve and uplift those less fortunate.... Ella grew up
> in a female-centered household, surrounded by a community
> of Christian women actively engaged in uplifting their families
> and communities. These women were as much concerned with
> enlightening the mind as they were with saving the soul.[83]

For Baker, it remained evident that there was "no model for collective or democratic decision making within the mainstream ministerial
tradition...[because]...most ministers expected to say their piece
and have their congregations obediently carry out their decisions."[84]
Throughout her life, Baker's critique of the male-centered leadership style of the black church viewed this flow of authority from the
pulpit to the pew "as a weakness, not a virtue," whereas "the socialization of women...meant that they practiced a more democratic and
decentralized style of religious service than male ministers did."[85]

Largely inspired by her religious upbringing as well as the moral
examples of the black churchwomen in her hometown, Baker's remarkable life was devoted to the welfare and uplift of the entire
African American community — male and female. Baker worked
closely with the most prominent African American men and women of
the century: W. E. B. Du Bois, Thurgood Marshall, George Schuyler,
Walter White, A. Philip Randolph, Martin Luther King, James For-
man, Stokely Carmichael, and Robert Moses — most often as the

"outsider within." Her friendships with legendary African American women of the era included Dorothy Height, Nannie Helen Burroughs, Pauli Murray, Mary McLeod Bethune, Septima Clark, Fannie Lou Hamer, and white radicals Anne Braden and Annie Stein. In the 1970s, Baker worked with the Puerto Rican Solidarity Movement and continued to nurture young activists. She inspired a younger generation of black feminists by illustrating a more secular rendition of the church-based activism demonstrated by the black women who were her role models.

"One of the major emphases of SNCC," Baker wrote in 1967, "was that of working with indigenous people, not working for them, but trying to develop their capacity for leadership." A larger glimpse of her unrelenting determination to nurture the capacity for leadership in new activists was evident on the campus of Shaw University, a historically black institution in North Carolina, during a pivotal Easter weekend in April 1960. According to Baker's biographer, Barbara Ransby:

> For many of the students, it was not until the gathering in Raleigh that they fully appreciated the national significance of their local activities. They felt honored by the presence of Dr. King, whom they had watched on television or read about in the black and mainstream press. He was a hero for most black people in 1960, and his presence gave the neophyte activists a clear sense of their own contribution to the growing civil rights movement. Baker was content to use King's celebrity to attract young people to the meeting, but she was determined that they take away something more substantial. Most of the student activists had never heard of Ella Baker before they arrived. Yet she, more than King, became the decisive force in their collective political future.... It was Baker, not King, who nurtured the student movement and helped to launch a new organization. It was Baker, not King, who offered the sit-in leaders a model of

organizing and an approach to politics that they found consistent with their own experience and would find invaluable in months and years to come.[86]

As before, in the final step of the moral biographical/autobiographical method, we pull together the common threads that comprise Baker's provocative life.

In her encounters with burgeoning young activists, Baker gave the students a sense of the importance of their actions.[87] As one of several keynote speakers at the Raleigh conference, Baker was the only woman to address a plenary session. When her opportunity came to speak, she urged the students to see their mission as extending beyond the immediate demand to end segregation. Baker helped them realize that the sit-in movement was part of an increasingly global struggle against myriad forms of injustice and oppression. She encouraged her participants to see themselves — not their parents, teachers, ministers, or recognized race leaders — as the main catalysts for change. She strived to pull student activists beyond the confines of the South and the nation to grapple with, and connect to, a large and complex political world.[88]

Ella Baker was not only a dynamic and influential teacher, mentor, and organizer, but also a leading symbol of women's rights of her day. She acted as an inspiration to many, including Rosa Parks. In every project she undertook, Baker broke new ground — as the first woman president of the New York branch of the NAACP, the only woman in the leadership core of SCLC. During her time in Harlem, she visited bars, bootblack parlors, and pool halls as part of her mission to increase NAACP membership. Even though those "forays into traditionally male domains [were] obvious gender transgressions . . . pushing the boundaries of acceptable behavior for a respectable, middle-class, married woman" of that era, Baker found such risks and efforts necessary in the cause of advancing civil rights.[89] She refused to believe that she was inferior due to race, class, or gender, nor did she accept the pervasive stereotypes of her era. She openly defied the dominant stereotype that would have required her to become a schoolteacher in the traditional sense. Rather, she made the entire United States her classroom, and her students became the students of a movement that encompassed thousands of persons, black and white alike. More than anything, she encouraged the students to think for themselves, and as a result, "because of its deepening irreverence for conventional standards... SNCC bestowed credibility and honor on women and girls who protested and fought back" in ways previously deemed as "unladylike."[90] Baker made it her special purpose to encourage young girls and women who had joined the movement to retain an active part in the struggle of the fight for civil rights. Baker also worked diligently to challenge and change the perspectives of men. "Many of these young men had been socialized into the dominant society's attitudes about gender and behaved in sexist, even macho ways," writes Ransby. "What is surprising is not the degree of conformity to social norms but rather the extent to which many young men in SNCC began to rethink and reject conventional notions of gender... redefining their own identities" largely under Baker's tutelage.[91] Although Baker never considered herself a feminist, it was evident to those around her that she was an intelligent, powerful woman who was never intimidated by her position as a female leader in a movement controlled by men. Ella Baker was a vital moral agent of social transformation.

Emancipatory Historiography

Emancipatory historiography explores specific episodes or critical junctures in the life history of a person when ethical formation and racial identity politics are ultimately redefined.[92] Emancipatory historiography merges history with ethics. Chronological events are read against an appreciation of black people's collective actions as agents, not victims. Emancipatory historiography interrogates black self-determination rather than accepting normative practices that deny black moral agency.

Emancipatory historiography makes sense of thoughts, actions, experiences, circumstances, and insights in the form of an ongoing story that is both historical and personal. The presupposition of this method is that all of us have a "faith narrative," a story of how our spiritual beliefs and values reveal themselves within our words, thoughts, and deeds. If we take as a given the fact that all people (especially people of African heritage) engage in a process of narrative structuring in order to locate logic and coherence in the midst of an existence that often seems illogical and incoherent, then the faith narrative accentuates an understanding of how to best represent God's will in that existence, although it is difficult to establish a story of our existence that satisfactorily reflects, much less makes sense of, the religious views and principles we might profess, yet ineffectively practice.

Emancipatory historiography is a crucial building block of our understanding of human history, particularly in contemporary times. In a society that is on the verge of willful historical amnesia on the one hand and that suffers from a collective short attention span on the other, creating a record of ethical formation and meaning and purpose is an urgent task. As the work of the philosopher Søren Kierkegaard suggests, the narrative model of history does not simply depend on the endless accumulation of data but includes the embrace of self-knowledge and how that knowledge leads to meaningful choices. As Kierkegaard is often quoted: "life must be understood backwards; but it must be lived forward," this is a realization that resonates deeply with the central concerns of the faith narrative. By tracing the principles that undergird one's sense of self and vocation as well as promoting critical inquiry about how those principles guide life, emancipatory historiography deconstructs and reconstructs faith narratives.

Emancipatory historiography, a method conceptualized by Katie Cannon, has four strata: theoretical analysis, systemic analysis, cultural disposition, and collective action.[93] First, *theoretical analysis* comprehends black experience in light of oppression. Second, *systemic analysis* is the investigation of how black women negotiated the dominant customs, laws, and structures of the public sphere (i.e., educational, economic, legal, and political institutions). Next, *cultural disposition* is the exploration of the shared consciousness that black women use in defining themselves and their actions — what blackness is, how it is embodied, and why it is necessary for communal as well as spiritual empowerment. Finally, *collective action* is the examination of the moral impetus or motivation that has led black people to devise ideologies, spaces, and movements that open greater venues of opportunity than previously deemed possible.

As a project for redemptive self-love of black women, emancipatory historiography is a critical sociohistorical tool. Its use may reveal not only the paralyzing effects of white privilege but also how individual resistance and collective action cultivate a more profound understanding of self-preservation and affirmation for black women.

Employing a Theoretical Analysis

Let us take the experience of Anita Hill as an example to which emancipatory historiography may be applied. As black feminist bell hooks contends:

> If Anita Hill had been a white woman accusing a black man of sexual harassment there would have been no television spectacle exposing her to the voyeuristic gaze of the masses. The forces of white-supremacist patriarchy would have demanded respect for her privacy, for her womanhood, a respect denied Anita Hill.[94]

The main concern for all womanists, black feminists as well as their allies, is that by "moving ourselves from manipulatable objects to self-empowered subjects, black women have by necessity threatened the status quo."[95] The crisis facing black women of all ages, backgrounds, and nationalities is a struggle to reclaim and redeem a notion of ourselves that refuses the limitations and lies that have been used to deny us dignity and, ultimately, love. The story of Anita Hill is of particular significance in this regard because it indicates the ongoing assault on black femininity by institutionalized structures of domination and individual acts of dehumanization. As Toni Morrison has asserted in her writings about the Clarence Thomas–Anita Hill controversy,

> Since neither the press nor the Senate Judiciary Committee would entertain seriously or exhaustively the truth of her accusations, she could be called any number or pair of discrediting terms and the contradictions would never be called into question, because, as a black woman, she was contradiction itself, irrationality in flesh.[96]

Despite her lauded career as a lawyer, professor, and civil servant, Hill's accomplishments and accolades were easily ignored by those interested in perpetuating the racism, sexism, classism, and paternalism of white supremacy. As Morrison develops her argument further, she indicates that Hill

> was portrayed as a lesbian who hated men *and* a vamp who could be ensnared and painfully rejected by them. She was a mixture heretofore not recognized in the glossary of racial tropes: an *intellectual* daughter of black *farmers;* a *black female* taking *offense;* a black *lady* repeating *dirty words.* Anita Hill's description of Thomas's behavior toward her did not ignite a careful search for the truth; her testimony simply produced an exchange of racial tropes.[97]

Executing a Systemic Analysis

In executing a systemic analysis, the researcher should look at the systems and organizations (including their laws, customs, politics, and sacred rhetoric) that empower people to perpetuate oppression. Returning to the Hill case, we recall that, in 1991, Thurgood Marshall, the first African American to be appointed to the United States

Supreme Court, decided to retire. Throughout his life, Justice Marshall epitomized the ideal of leadership in the legal fight for civil rights. He led the NAACP's historic battle against racial segregation in the *Brown vs. Board of Education of Topeka* case in the 1950s, which sought to desegregate America's public schools. The landmark decision was a major catalyst for the modern civil rights movement and gave Thurgood Marshall national prominence as an advocate for civil rights. In 1967, President Lyndon Johnson appointed him to the Supreme Court. Twenty-four years later, as Justice Marshall prepared to retire from the highest court in the land, a decidedly more conservative political atmosphere dominated national politics. President George H. W. Bush saw Justice Marshall's retirement as an opportunity to appoint a more conservative judge to the Supreme Court. His choice was Clarence Thomas, a forty-three-year-old conservative African American from Pinpoint, Georgia. As a black conservative, Thomas served the Bush agenda perfectly. He would maintain the racial makeup of the court, but add another conservative voice on decisions involving affirmative action and abortion.

President Bush's nomination of Clarence Thomas was immediately controversial. Many African American and civil rights organizations, including the NAACP, the National Bar Association (the African American counterpart to the American Bar Association), and the Urban League, opposed the Thomas nomination. These organizations feared that Thomas's conservative stance on issues such as affirmative action would reverse the civil rights movement's monumental gains that Justice Marshall had fought so hard to achieve. Women's groups such as the National Organization for Women (NOW) were equally concerned that if appointed to the high court, Clarence Thomas would rule to overturn *Roe v. Wade.* The legal community also voiced apprehension about Thomas's clear lack of experience since he had only served two years as a federal judge.

Despite the countless voices of anger, the Thomas nomination proceeded to the Senate Judiciary Committee's confirmation hearings.

The first few days of the hearings were relatively uneventful. When asked about his stance on legalized abortion, Thomas claimed that he had not formulated an opinion, and the issue was dropped. After a few more days of outside testimony, it appeared as if the Senate committee would easily confirm the Thomas nomination. The committee split its vote, however — seven to seven, and the nomination went to the Senate without a clear recommendation.

When the nomination moved to the floor of the Senate, it took a sudden and dramatic turn when Anita Hill, a black female law professor at the University of Oklahoma, came forward with accusations that Clarence Thomas had sexually harassed her. Hill had worked for Thomas years earlier when he was head of the Equal Employment Opportunity Commission. During the nomination hearings, Hill testified that Thomas harassed her with inappropriate discussion of sexual acts and pornographic films after she rebuffed his invitations to date him. Adding insult to injury, while Thomas made Hill a target of his sexual conquest, he was married to a white woman. As this story grew increasingly more lewd, the nationwide media frenzy quickly arose around Thomas's denials and Hill's allegations. When Thomas testified about Hill's claims before the Senate Judiciary Committee, he called the hearings "a high-tech lynching for uppity blacks." This incident quickly deteriorated into a case of "he said/she said" and, in the end, the Senate voted 52–48 to confirm Clarence Thomas as associate justice of the Supreme Court.

To the many people who believed Anita Hill's claims or opposed the Thomas nomination on other grounds, Thomas's appointment was a defeat. Yet, the Anita Hill–Clarence Thomas controversy had other long-term consequences. First and foremost, the national awareness about sexual harassment in the workplace heightened considerably during the 1990s. According to Equal Employment Opportunity Commission filings during the decade, the number of sexual harassment cases more than doubled, from 6,127 in 1991 to 15,342 in 1996. Over the same period, awards paid to victims under federal laws nearly quadrupled, from $7.7 million to $27.8 million. Another repercussion of the Hill-Thomas controversy was the increased involvement of women in politics. The news media heralded the 1992 election year as the "Year of the Woman" when a record number of women ran for public office and won. In the U.S. Senate, eleven women ran and five won seats, including one incumbent candidate. In the House of Representatives, twenty-four women won new seats. Many commentators saw this increase as a direct reaction to the Thomas nomination. His appointment dismayed many women, who felt that a Senate that was 98 percent male did not take Anita Hill's allegations seriously.

Anita Hill's charge of sexual harassment against Clarence Thomas, some observers have predicted, was the catalyst for a growing tension and mistrust in the daily interactions between men and women in the workplace and a surge of sexual harassment claims and lawsuits. It can be justifiably argued that there was incredible anxiety over sexual politics long before Anita Hill was subpoenaed to testify before the Senate Judiciary Committee. This level of apprehension was due to how many men feel about the issue of sexual harassment, and the level of concern many women feel not only about this issue, but also about their rights in the workplace, the ineffectualness of their representation in Congress, and especially the virulence of certain stereotypes about black women that many men and women hold. Whereas many men are seemingly conflicted about these limits, most women do not share this dismay about the precise boundaries of sexual harassment. Why would a committee of wealthy, well-connected white male politicians assume that quitting a job or refusing another good job is the proper option for women facing sexual harassment — this after several senators "proved" that Anita Hill's job at Education was "secure"? Are women who have not personally experienced sexual harassment really so judgmental of women who have? And does Republican Senator Orrin Hatch really believe a man would have to be a "complete pervert" to say the things Anita Hill alleges Clarence Thomas said to her?

To show how truly absurd the events surrounding Thomas's nomination trial became, the late Senator Strom Thurmond, a renowned racist as well as a legendary womanizer, publicly came to the defense of Clarence Thomas by stating that Hill's charges against the nominee were essentially a conspiracy fueled by feminists and other liberals who hated Thomas for his conservative politics. When the nation's most infamous segregationist and sexist philanderer is his strongest supporter, what personal credibility and integrity could Thomas have? More than anything else, this unholy union between Thurmond and Thomas marked the worst possible social and political identification for this controversial black nominee by his many opponents. Furthermore, given the recent revelation by Mrs. Essie Mae Washington-Williams that she was the biracial daughter of the senator and the Thurmond family's African American maid adds another lurid dimension to this story. Even as Thurmond stood judgment over the reported sexual misconduct of Clarence Thomas, the senator had spent the majority of his adult life keeping the existence of his black daughter a secret for the sake of his political aspirations and personal reputation. If Thurmond's sexual transgressions had been subject to the same level of scrutiny as imposed on the Hill-Thomas controversy, the fact that Thurmond's biracial child was the product of his own statutory rape of a black female teenager employed by his family would have been an important indictment of the dangerous intersection of race, sex, and power in America. Unfortunately, this debate never occurred during Thurmond's lifetime, and this illustration of Thurmond as both a racist hypocrite and a sexual predator was never dealt with in any meaningful way.

The impetus for emancipatory historiography is to overturn the forces that conspire to silence the protests of women subjected to various social ills and injustice. The conservative senators' (namely, Strom Thurmond, Arlen Specter, and Orrin Hatch) "concern" was about why Anita Hill did not file a complaint against Thomas sooner is absurd in light of the serious punishment many women receive when they do speak up. The senators' judgment of when women do or do not feel "secure" enough to leave a job is unsound. And the senators' assertion that a woman "should" consider leaving a job as a way of handling sexual harassment is a violation of the U.S. Constitution. The real travesty of the "Anita Hill trial" is that the right of any citizen to be free from sexual harassment was put in false opposition to the right of an American citizen to be free from racial discrimination. Rather than clarifying and strengthening such legal principles, which is what happens in an honest clash of rights, the process diminished all.

If we use emancipatory historiography, the Anita Hill–Clarence Thomas controversy illuminates many of the central tensions of life in contemporary America. Justice Thomas's nomination to replace Justice Marshall prompted new thoughts on the accomplishments of the modern civil rights movement by sparking more debate about affirmative action policies as well as meaningful African American leadership. Even as Clarence Thomas was being sworn in as a Supreme Court justice, black America was severely wounded by growing tensions and mistrust in the daily interactions between black men and women who had been deeply embarrassed by the "airing of dirty laundry" in front of the whole world. Meanwhile, Anita Hill's accusations heightened public awareness of sexual harassment in the workplace and black women's unequal representation in the political sphere as well as popular culture, an issue that helped to renew interest in women's rights issues within American society. Moreover, the ensuing media frenzy surrounding the event marked a new trend of obsessive and often tabloid-style coverage that has only worsened through subsequent news events such as the O. J. Simpson murder trial, the Monica Lewinsky–Bill Clinton sex scandal, the Kobe Bryant rape trial, and the Michael Jackson child sex abuse trial. As significant as these events are on their own terms, historians, sociologists, journalists, and other students of the late twentieth century will always turn to the Anita Hill–Clarence Thomas controversy in order to understand race relations, gender politics, and media influences in America at the dawn of

the twenty-first century. As demonstrated above, emancipatory historiography might serve in this and other instances to begin examining
the multiplicity of moral factors in such contemporary controversies.

Articulating the Cultural Disposition

By inverting the fundamental premise of stereotypes and social oppression, Anita Hill's testimony about Clarence Thomas's sexual
harassment was equal parts *revelation* and *revolution*. In her work *Dark
Continent of Our Bodies,* black feminist scholar E. Frances White emphasizes that revelation and revolution are inherently bound together
in what she calls "Black counterdiscourses" to the dominant historical narrative within American society. Explaining the significance of
black counterdiscourses, White states:

> they expose the ways that race, gender, sexuality, and class cat-
> egories intertwine and transform each other. Categories such
> as race and gender are created to help the world make sense
> to us. These categories do not exist "out there" in the world.
> Rather, they are analytical categories that are always structured
> hierarchically and that have real consequences for real people.[98]

The central focus of emancipatory historiography as redemptive self-
love is to chronicle the deliberate efforts of black women to challenge
hegemonic perspectives. Even as black women grapple with and interrogate slave narratives and moral biographies/autobiographies as
historical resources, it is still difficult for many black women to address
the pejorative circumstances of their current existences. To borrow an
insight drawn from James Baldwin:

> History, as nearly no one seems to know, is not merely something
> to be read. And it does not refer merely, or even principally,
> to the past. On the contrary, the great force of history comes

from the fact that we carry it within us, are unconsciously controlled by it in many ways, and history is literally *present* in all that we do.[99]

The intolerable burden of American history weighs heavily on the bodies, souls, and minds of black women. It is imperative that such a reality is addressed in a straightforward and meaningful way. As the living, breathing victims of slavery, racial segregation, and ongoing white supremacy, black women need to be mindful that "when wounded individuals come together in groups to make change our collective struggle is often undermined by all that has not been dealt with emotionally."[100] The counterdiscourse to modern history that can enable black women to tell their truths and live their lives is the ultimate goal of emancipatory historiography for womanist ethics.

Anyone who is honestly and wholeheartedly committed to liberation in its broadest terms needs to engage in a project that has redemptive self-love at its core. In her classic anthology *The Black Woman*, the late black feminist scholar Toni Cade Bambara asserts that

revolution begins with the self, in the self. The individual, the basic revolutionary unit, must be purged of poison and lies that assault the ego and threaten the heart, that hazard the next larger revolutionary unit — the couple or pair, that jeopardize the still larger unit — the family . . . that put the entire movement in peril. We make many false starts because we have been programmed to depend on white models or white interpretations of non-white models, so we don't even ask the correct questions, much less begin to move in a correct direction.[101]

Acknowledging the paradigm shift that Toni Cade Bambara advocates also means systematically dismantling the conditions that have made black women perennially denigrated figures in American society. Engaging in such a revolutionary transformation of black women's sense

of self makes structural and systemic changes — from politics, law, eco-
nomics, religion, education, science, etc. — more feasible. Sociologist
Daphne Wiggins contends:

> Womanists are not wed to biblical authority that is predicated
> on the Bible's being inerrant or infallible....Most have not re-
> jected the Bible or Christianity in total, as some radical feminist
> theologians have. They value and advocate for the physical and
> spiritual salvation of the family, redistribution of wealth, goods,
> and services in American society, and the end of race, sex,
> and class supremacy. In addition, they are devoted to articu-
> lating a theological liberative position for women even when it
> might be at odds with a black male perspective on what would
> enhance African American existence. They address society's de-
> humanization and oppression of black women. Finally, they resist
> grand narratives of history which obsfucate particular realities
> and tend to universal experience from the dominant group's
> perspective.[102]

As Wiggins suggests, womanism both demands and depends upon
a radical reinterpretation of all elements of contemporary society,
especially history, to promote the overall goal of human liberation.
Emancipatory historiography serves as the means to those ends.

Recovering Collective Action

Recovering collective action is the most critical step in the emancipatory historiographical method. In black women's experience,
the victories won and defiance with which oppression is met gets
overshadowed by stigma, hopelessness, and victimization. The Hill-
Thomas controversy offers a particularly poignant and invaluable
example. As the level of debate and scandal soared to unimaginable
heights, black women nationwide wondered if or when anyone would
rally to the defense of black women in light of the excruciating attacks
Anita Hill suffered throughout her testimony. For instance, amidst the

ongoing public debate about the Hill-Thomas hearings, Deborah Gray White pondered whether she was being forced

> to choose between my blackness and my womanhood. How could I side with one part of my identity without denying the other? Where were black women's voices? Where were *my* advocates? Where were the people who were supposed to explain to the country who *I* was, to explain why *I* felt as I did, to deal with *my* conflicts? Why were they silent?[103]

White received the answer to her queries on November 17, 1991, when several hundred black women banded together under the slogan of "African American Women in Defense of Ourselves" to protest Thomas's seating on the bench of the U.S. Supreme Court. Even as the white women who constituted the so-called Third Wave of American feminism sought to use the Anita Hill story as cause célèbre, it was the slow but steady emergence of organized rallies, academic conferences, published works, and critique by black women and men that condemned the death-dealing circumstances endured by Professor Hill and untold numbers of other black women. Eventually even Hill was able to find the strength and resolve to write her memoirs, *Speaking Truth to Power.* Hill was able to withstand the abuses and reproaches of right-wing opponents and other supporters of the status quo, but others, especially black women, also joined together to struggle against the ravages of racism, sexism, classism, and all other forms of oppression in our time, in a hopeful act for generations to come.

Practical Strategies for Critical Engagement in Historiography

Womanist emancipatory historiography lends itself to an analysis of self-narratives derived from the realization that the more one travels to a world of another, the more one learns about oneself. The womanist ethical model of critically engaging black women's life stories and faith narratives lends itself to the systematic interpretation of faith narratives while, at the same time, allowing the interpreter to work with self-identity texts (such as journals, diaries, letters, or autobiographies).

But the study of black women's life stories and faith narratives also helps the students and researchers learn to chart one's own faith narratives in a quest to discern how certain contestable ethical issues have impacted their faith formation. The faith narrative articulates the application of a Christian ethical perspective.

The Womanist Faith Narrative and Theoethical Credo

The faith narrative approach, or theoethical credo, is a historically reflective exercise, incorporating backgrounds, conditions, and contexts that seem to shape the development of what one believes in light of salient experiences in their life history. The faith narrative/theoethical credo exercise is accomplished by attending to the following four criteria:

- *Theoethical Analysis* — Describe a key moment in your life in which you have experienced cognitive dissonance. Then discuss how this critical moment required you to "mine" the events, resources, and discourses that you have found influential in shaping your faith narrative thus far and explain how you can reconcile the disparate issues that emerge within your personal story of spiritual and ethical formation.

- *Questioning the Past* — What has been the metaethical problem with which you have constantly struggled? (In other words, what causes you grave concern? How does it continue to manifest itself? And why does it continue to happen?) Be sure to emphasize how this problem impacts your *ethos* (values), *pathos* (feelings), *logos* (reasoning), and *theos* (ultimate concerns). In light of your theoethical analysis and metaethical problem, what is the historical question that guides your spiritual and ethical formation?

♦ *Moral Inventory of Causation* — Write a brief inventory of your historical perspective on causation (the relationship between cause and effect) in light of the moral question you confront by focusing on the following factors which lead to the development of each person's moral understanding: (*a*) *cultural context and social location* — What are the cultural/social bases for how you understand what it means to be "religious"? (*b*) *religious heritage* — How were you introduced to your faith (not just formal religion but that which was privileged as sacred), and what appealed to you most about your faith tradition? (*c*) *spiritual-ethical formation and personal growth* — How do your feelings, ideas, and perceptions of that which is sacred and most important in your life reflect the immediacy as well as importance of social action in your life? and (*d*) *vocation as a call to ministry and/or social action* — How did you first realize your personal calling or purpose in life? How have you instilled the virtues of radical subjectivity, traditional communalism, redemptive self-love, and critical engagement in your role as a justice-making agent?

♦ *Constructing an ethic of liberation* — Create and outline a feasible constructive ethic that you might espouse incorporating and/or differentiating the discourses of womanist ethicists (and other liberationists). By posing critical questions about how you came to develop your current beliefs, devise a systematic approach for reconstructing your faith narrative. Toward this end, it is important to name what possible contributions and implications your faith narrative might have for the task of a liberating theological ethic and how it will shape not only your formation but also the ways in which it could help resolve a specific dilemma within the thinking, being, and doing of the privileged and dispossessed within contemporary society.

As the faith narrative/theoethical credo exercise shows, the ability to articulate a thoroughgoing inventory includes the ability to move beyond assessment or analysis of a historical context in order to do constructive ethics. That task requires identifying, differentiating, and using concepts provided by other nondominant/normative perspectives and prioritizing these worm's-view perspectives as an alternative view for seeing oneself, and then constructing in communicable form to this same alternative perspective one's own theoethical position. This form of interactive articulation involves the womanist ethical task of demonstrating the ability to converse with, engage in dialogue with, respect, and construct one's own views in ways that mutual communication with others, especially the marginalized, occurs. Ultimately, the evaluative component of the faith narrative/theoethical credo includes the ability to express how one's ethical perspective informs, assists, and critiques human decisions and actions either as agency that is justice-making or agency that is complicit with the oppression of another. This exercise is not a case study or autobiography per se; nonetheless, it requires the annunciation of the value of ethical discourse in the development of one's own trajectory for charting one's progress toward liberative change and undoing what history might have done.

Conclusion

The Why Crisis of Womanist Ethics

[handwritten margin note: how do more methods logier make their way or not into black churches?]

Womanist scholars have long attested to the import of black women's musings and life lessons. I believe, however, that they serve as more than just a muse for black people. Rather, the narratives of black women's lives catalog existences and experiences of moral tenacity. They produce a constructive moral ethic that goes beyond death-dealing stereotypes and the dominant systems that perpetuate them. In examining black women's real-lived experiences as a repository of moral wisdom, we may come to some understanding of the degree to which womanist ethics helps record, imagine, and aid women in their journey toward liberation. In this regard, womanist ethics fills in the gaps of Christian feminist theological ethics and black liberation theology to make visible a theology that cannot be subsumed by either yet that renders pertinent the moral judgments of both.

Womanist ethics is not only for black women or scholars but for anyone committed to the task of social justice and self-empowerment. The methods here, though representative, are in no way definitive. We need many more methods that can be delineated from or inspired by the works of womanist ethicists. Indeed, the harvest is plentiful, but the laborers are few! Further mining of this vast motherlode will encourage scholars and students to openly examine difficult material, facilitate understanding between members of unequal social groups, and provide a framework for engaging critically with various forms of oppression.

After having explored the literary, sociological, historiographical, and pedagogical approaches for doing womanist ethics, the answer to the "why crisis" for doing womanist ethics should be clear. But the willingness to restate the presumably obvious when doing work from the perspectives of black women is essential for anyone who wishes to do this justice-making work. In an academy, church, and world that declares that all the blacks are men and all the women are white, to quote Gloria Hull, we need those who are brave and courageous, audacious and willful, to make visible those who have been rendered invisible.

Why is it essential for this work to be done by the courageous and audacious? Whenever one seeks to do work on behalf of a community rather than an academy, it is risky. Academics might regard it as trendy and practical, while community folk might be suspicious and offended by its intellectual orientation. Heralding any approach or theory espoused by black women as its authors and experts is suspect — for this work will always be rebuffed with the snub, "What authority do black women have?" or "Why should we dumb down the discipline by allowing black women to speak to their concerns?"

The truth remains that black women are only relevant to explain, legitimate, or ensure the logic of men and other women's lives, security, comfort, and success. Black women's lives have no meaning in and of themselves outside of this utilitarian end. Simply put, for them to be relevant is for them to be useful. Along their scholarly-activist journey and epistemological formation, womanist ethicists are forever aware of this fact. And so, too, should their allies be. But whether we hearken to literary protagonist Celie's assertion that the world would be a better place if God and God's creation saw the world through the eyes of black women; or to Sojourner Truth's pithy retort that if it took women to turn the world upside down, it will take women to turn it right side up again; or to Walker's warning that the soul we save may be our own, womanist ethics guides us to a truer and fuller sense of what it means to be in right-relationship with everyone as it furthers our individual efforts toward self-determination, mutuality, social liberation, and spiritual empowerment. And for the field of Christian social ethics, the work of womanist ethics is an essential, not oppositional, discourse that seeks to build upon previously underutilized resources in order to fulfill its goal of surveying the range of human agency, the various contexts of human relationship, and the effects of human actions. However, as a liberative discourse womanist ethics critiques normative ethics' preoccupation with right and wrong as determined by divine, natural, or governmental law and order. Instead, womanist ethics ascertains the just and the unjust in personal, social, and divine wills. Womanist ethical analysis makes evident how patterns of human conduct, as manifested in the actions of black women, address and answer the questions of agency, relationships, and quest for liberative action, while offering a centered critique of the canonical, theological, and philosophical sources in normative Christian ethics. Thus, womanist ethics reveals the inner workings of the moral crises that oppressive ideologies create for black women and the various entrapments in which they are placed. In the moral resources of radical subjectivity, traditional communalism, redemptive self-love, and critical engagement womanist ethics offers a new set of methodological tools that help us to not only mine the motherlode of black women's moral wisdom but also may change ourselves in the process.

Notes

Preface

1. Alice Walker, *The Color Purple* (New York: Washington Square Press, 1982), 175.

Introduction

1. Katie G. Cannon, as quoted in Sara Lawrence-Lightfoot, *I've Known Rivers: Lives of Loss and Liberation* (Reading, MA: Addison Wesley, 1994), 59.

2. Margaret Farley, "Ethics and Moral Theologies," in *The Dictionary of Feminist Theologies,* ed. Letty M. Russell and J. Shannon Clarkson (Louisville: Westminster John Knox, 1996), 88–89.

3. Alice Walker, *In Search of Our Mothers' Gardens: Womanist Prose* (San Diego: Harcourt Brace Jovanovich, 1983), xi–xii.

4. Katie G. Cannon, "The Emergence of Black Feminist Consciousness," in *Feminist Interpretation of the Bible,* ed. Letty M. Russell (Louisville: Westminster, 1985), 30–40.

5. Emilie Townes, "Womanist Ethics," in *The Dictionary of Feminist Theologies,* ed. Letty M. Russell and J. Shannon Clarkson (Louisville: Westminster John Knox, 1996), 91.

6. Katie G. Cannon, in Cheryl J. Sanders et al., "Roundtable Discussion: Christian Ethics and Theology in Womanist Perspective," in *Journal of Feminist Studies in Religion* 5 (1989): 92.

7. Cheryl Townsend Gilkes, in Cheryl J. Sanders et al., "Roundtable Discussion: Christian Ethics and Theology in Womanist Perspective," in *Journal of Feminist Studies in Religion* 5 (1989): 108–9.

8. Barbara Christian, *Black Feminist Criticism: Perspectives on Black Women Writers* (New York: Pergamon Press, 1985), 144.

9. Michele Jacques, "Testimony as Embodiment: Telling the Truth and Shaming the Devil," *Journal of the Interdenominational Theological Center* 22, no. 2 (Spring 1995): 145.

10. Emilie Townes, as quoted in Gary David Comstock, *A Whosoever Church: Welcoming Lesbians and Gay Men into African American Congregations* (Louisville: Westminster John Knox Press, 2001), 225.

Chapter 1: Black Women's Literary Analysis

1. Katie G. Cannon, *Katie's Canon: Womanism and the Soul of the Black Community* (New York: Continuum, 1995), 60.

2. Karen Baker-Fletcher, "Tar Baby and Womanist Theology," *Theology Today* 50, no. 1 (April 1993): 29.

3. Barbara Christian, *Black Feminist Criticism: Perspectives on Black Women Writers* (New York: Pergamon Press, 1985), 13.

4. Cannon, *Katie's Canon*, 77.

5. bell hooks, in Cheryl J. Sanders et al., "Roundtable Discussion: Christian Ethics and Theology in Womanist Perspective," in *Journal of Feminist Studies in Religion* 5 (1989): 103.

6. Katie G. Cannon, *Black Womanist Ethics* (Atlanta: Scholars Press, 1988), 76.

7. See Joy Elizabeth Browne, "Theology and Literary Criticism in the Womanist Mode," *Journal of the Interdenominational Theological Center* 22, no. 2 (Spring 1995): 115–28; see also Cheryl Townsend Gilkes, "A Conscious Connection to All That Is: The Color Purple as Subversive and Critical Ethnography," in *Embracing the Spirit: Womanist Perspectives on Hope, Salvation, and Transformation,* ed. Emilie Townes (Maryknoll, NY: Orbis Books, 1997), 275–96; Youtha Hardman-Cromwell, "Living in the Intersection of Womanism and Afrocentrism: Black Women Writers," in *Living the Intersection: Womanism and Afrocentrism in Theology* (Minneapolis: Fortress, 1995), 115–20.

8. Cannon, *Black Womanist Ethics,* 184.

9. Christian, *Black Feminist Criticism.*

10. Browne, "Theology and Literary Criticism in the Womanist Mode," 115.

11. Emilie Townes, in Cheryl J. Sanders et al., "Roundtable Discussion: Christian Ethics and Theology in Womanist Perspective," in *Journal of Feminist Studies in Religion* 5 (1989): 95–96.

12. Suzette A. Henke, *Shattered Subjects: Trauma and Testimony in Women's Life-Writing* (New York: St. Martin's Press, 1998), 103.

13. Hortense Spillers, "Interstices: A Small Drama of Words," as quoted in AnaLouise Keating, *Women Reading Women Writing: Self-Invention in Paula Gunn Allen, Gloria Anzaldúa and Audre Lorde* (Philadelphia: Temple University Press, 1996), 155–56.

14. Drucilla Cornell, *Transformations: Recollective Imagination and Sexual Difference*, as quoted in Keating, *Women Reading Women Writing*, 159.

15. Toni Morrison, "Behind the Making of the Black Book," *Black World* 23 (February 1974): 88.

16. Carolyn Medine, "Memory, Narrative, and Peacemaking in Toni Morrison's Fiction" (paper presentation, Annual Meeting of the American Academy of Religion, Atlanta, November 23, 2003), 8.

17. Molefi Kete Asante, *The Afrocentric Idea* (Philadelphia: Temple University Press, 1998), 17.

18. Medine, "Memory, Narrative, and Peacemaking in Toni Morrison's Fiction," 7.

19. Michele Jacques, "Testimony as Embodiment: Telling the Truth and Shaming the Devil," *Journal of the Interdenominational Theological Center* 22, no. 2 (Spring 1995): 129.

20. Ibid., 130.

21. Ibid.

22. "A Conversation, Gloria Naylor and Toni Morrison," *Southern Review* 21, no. 3 (July 1985): 593.

23. Medine, "Memory, Narrative, and Peacemaking in Toni Morrison's Fiction," 9.

24. Karen Baker-Fletcher, "Womanism, Afro-centrism, and the Reconstruction of Black Womanhood," *Journal of the Interdenominational Theological Center* 22, no. 2 (Spring 1995): 195.

25. Alice Walker, *The Color Purple* (New York: Washington Square Press, 1982), 179.

26. Alice Walker, *In Search of Our Mothers' Gardens: Womanist Prose* (New York: Harcourt Brace Jovanovich, 1983), xi.

27. Gilkes, "A Conscious Connection to All That Is," 280.

28. Townes, "Roundtable Discussion," 96.

29. Christian, *Black Feminist Criticism*, 176.

30. Baker-Fletcher, "Tar Baby and Womanist Theology," 37.

31. Emilie Townes, "Womanist Ethics," in *The Dictionary of Feminist Theologies*, ed. Letty M. Russell and J. Shannon Clarkson (Louisville: Westminster John Knox, 1996), 91.

32. Maura A. Ryan, "Virtue," in Russell and Clarkson, *Dictionary of Feminist Theologies*, 312.

33. Katie G. Cannon, "Womanist Virtue," 313.

34. Ibid.

35. Cannon, *Black Womanist Ethics*, 77.

36. Cheryl A. Kirk-Duggan, *Exorcising Evil: A Womanist Perspective on the Spirituals* (Maryknoll, NY: Orbis Books, 1997), 146.

37. Cannon, "Womanist Virtue," 313.

38. Cannon, *Black Womanist Ethics,* 144.

39. Ibid., 77.

40. Cheryl Townsend Gilkes, "Roundtable Discussion," 109.

41. The steps used in this womanist literary method of virtue ethics are culled from and inspired by Katie G. Cannon's unpublished "Womanist Methodology Model."

42. Baker-Fletcher, "Womanism, Afro-centrism, and the Reconstruction of Black Womanhood," 188.

43. Cannon, *Black Womanist Ethics,* 127.

44. Ibid., 124.

45. Baker-Fletcher, "Womanism, Afro-centrism, and the Reconstruction of Black Womanhood," 183.

46. Zora Neale Hurston, *Mules and Men* (New York: Vintage, 1903, 1982), 34.

47. Cannon, *Black Womanist Ethics,* 126.

48. Ibid., 128.

49. Ibid.

50. Ibid.

51. Jacques, "Testimony as Embodiment," 129.

52. Ibid., 144.

53. Hurston, *Their Eyes Were Watching God,* 183.

54. Jacques, "Testimony as Embodiment," 130–31.

55. Ibid., 130.

56. Ibid.

57. Ibid., 145.

58. For a more in-depth look at black identity politics, see bell hooks, *Yearning: Race, Gender, and Cultural Politics* (Boston: South End Press, 1990).

59. Joan M. Martin, "The Notion of Difference for Emerging Womanist Ethics: The Writings of Audre Lorde and bell hooks," *Journal of Feminist Studies in Religion* 9, nos. 1–2 (Spring–Fall 1993): 43.

60. When taking their writings into account collectively, black women's textualities should be read as a "series of boundary crossings and not as a fixed geographical, ethnically, or nationally bound category of writing." Carole Boyce Davies, *Black Women, Writing and Identity: Migrations of the Subject* (New York: Routledge, 1994), 4.

61. W. E. B. Du Bois, *The Souls of Black Folk* (New York: Vintage, 1903, 1982), 8–9.

62. For a full exploration of ontological blackness, see Victor Anderson, *Beyond Ontological Blackness: An Essay on African American Religious and Cultural Criticism* (New York: Continuum, 1995).

63. Stacey Floyd-Thomas and Laura Gillman, "Subverting Forced Identities, Violent Acts and the Narrativity of Race: A Diasporic Analysis of Black

Women's Radical Subjectivity in Three Novel Acts," *Journal of Black Studies* 32, no. 5 (2002): 528–56.

64. Maria Lugones, "Playfulness, 'World'-Travelling, and Loving Perception," in *Making Face, Making Soul*, ed. Gloria Anzaldúa (San Francisco: Aunt Lute Foundation, 1990), 401.

Chapter 2: A Sociology of Black Liberation

1. The study of black culture and religious life and its attention to the politics of race in social scientific research is explicitly discussed in classic black sociological and anthropological texts: C. Eric Lincoln's *Black Muslims in America* (Boston: Beacon Press, 1961), W. E. B. Du Bois's *The Souls of Black Folk* (New York: Vintage, 1903, 1982), and Zora Neale Hurston's *Mules and Men* (New York: Vintage, 1903, 1982).

2. Robert Staples as cited in Marcia Y. Riggs, *Awake, Arise, and Act: A Womanist Call for Black Liberation* (Cleveland: Pilgrim, 1994).

3. Riggs, *Awake, Arise, and Act*, 2.

4. For further sociological critiques supporting this claim, see Joyce A. Ladner, ed., *The Death of White Sociology* (New York: Random House, 1973); Patricia Hill Collins, *Black Feminist Thought: Knowledge, Consciousness, and the Politics of Empowerment* (Boston: Unwin Hyman, 1990); Margaret Andersen, *Thinking about Women: Sociological Perspectives on Sex and Gender* (Boston: Allyn and Bacon, 1983, 2002); and Cheryl Townsend Gilkes, *"If It Wasn't for the Women . . . ": Black Women's Experience and Womanist Culture in Church and Community* (Maryknoll, NY: Orbis Books, 2001).

5. Gloria Hull, Pat Bell Scott, and Barbara Smith, *All the Women Are White, All the Blacks Are Men, But Some of Us Are Brave* (Old Westbury, NY: Feminist Press, 1982).

6. Riggs, *Awake, Arise, and Act*, 10.

7. Ibid., 8.

8. Ibid., 12.

9. Katie G. Cannon, *Katie's Canon: Womanism and the Soul of the Black Community* (New York: Continuum, 1995), 144.

10. See Marcia Y. Riggs, *Plenty Good Room: Women Versus Male Power in the Black Church* (Cleveland: Pilgrim, 2003), and Traci C. West, *Wounds of the Spirit: Black Women, Violence and Resistance Ethics* (New York: New York University Press, 1999).

11. For a detailed introduction to metaethics and its implications for black preaching, see Katie G. Cannon, *Teaching Preaching: Isaac Rufus Clark and Black Sacred Rhetoric* (New York: Continuum, 2002).

12. The difference between a participatory learner and a participant-observer is that a participatory learner allows her findings and her orientation

to be informed by the knowledge or agency of the research group. To the contrary, the participant-observer participates not to be taught by the researchers but rather to test out or exert one's own agency to generate knowledge.

13. See Scenario B in Riggs, *Awake, Arise, and Act,* 68–69.

14. Moynihan's research serves as a prime example of how sociologists projected pathologies of unstable family and perpetual poverty onto blacks rather than reflected the pervasive damage of these factors to all Americans. For an in-depth exploration of how the publication of the Moynihan Report coincided with demonization of black women as the root cause of black pathology, namely black men's emasculation, broken families, and the cycle of poverty, see Sheila Radford-Hill, *Further to Fly: Black Women and the Politics of Empowerment* (Minneapolis: University of Minnesota Press, 2000).

15. Toinette Eugene, "Moral Values and Black Womanists," *Journal of Religious Thought* 45, no. 4 (1988): 24.

16. Riggs, *Awake, Arise, and Act,* 4.

17. Emilie Townes, ed., *A Troubling in My Soul: Womanist Perspectives on Evil and Suffering* (Maryknoll, NY: Orbis Books, 1993), 2.

18. Jacquelyn Grant, "Black Theology and the Black Woman," in *Black Theology: A Documentary History, 1966–1979* (Maryknoll, NY: Orbis Books, 1993), 1:331.

19. Womanist scholars have insisted upon emphasizing a black woman interpretation of sacred stories regarding "women of color" (like Hagar, the Egyptian woman in Genesis, the Queen of Sheba, and others) reclaiming and redeeming women's experience from the grips of a "sacred world" dominated by ethnocentrism and male power structures. For examples of this, see Renita J. Weems, *I Asked for Intimacy: Stories of Blessings, Betrayals, and Birthings* (San Diego: LuraMedia, 1993) and *Battered Love: Marriage, Sex, and Violence in the Hebrew Prophets* (Minneapolis: Fortress Press, 1995); Clarice J. Martin, "The *Haustafeln* (Household Codes) in African American Biblical Interpretation: 'Free Slaves' and 'Subordinate Women,'" in *Stony the Way We Trod,* ed. C. H. Felder (Minneapolis: Fortress, 1991), 206–31; and Delores Williams, *Sisters in the Wilderness: The Challenge of Womanist God-Talk* (Maryknoll, NY: Orbis Books, 1993).

20. Riggs, *Awake, Arise, and Act,* 82.

21. Cannon, *Katie's Canon,* 139.

22. Traces of the Dance of Redemption methodology have also appeared within the research of womanist sociologists of religion Carol Duncan, Cheryl Townsend-Gilkes, and Daphne Wiggins.

23. Beverly Wildung Harrison, *Making the Connections: Essays in Feminist Social Ethics,* ed. Carol S. Robb (Boston: Beacon, 1985), 249.

24. Cannon, *Katie's Canon,* 141.

25. Riggs, *Awake, Arise, and Act,* xi.

26. Cannon, *Katie's Canon*, 142.

27. Harrison, *Making the Connections*, 240.

28. Deborah Austin, "In the Middle of Everyday Life: The Spaces Black Clergywomen Create," *Journal of the Interdenominational Theological Center* 22, no. 2 (Spring 1995): 227.

29. Riggs, *Awake, Arise, and Act*, 59.

30. Harrison, *Making the Connections*, 263.

31. Key figures in psychology such as Erik Erikson (1963), Carl Jung (1958), Gordon Allport (1950), Jean Piaget (1954), Lawrence Kohlberg (1963), and James W. Fowler (1981) have all done various amounts of research on faith development, within which the faith formation of black women have gone uncharted. For an example, see Fowler's *Stages of Faith: The Psychology of Human Development and the Quest for Meaning* (New York: Harper & Row, 1981).

32. Charlene Spretnak, *The Politics of Women's Spirituality* (New York: Anchor Press, 1982).

33. Ada María Isasi-Díaz, *En la Lucha — In the Struggle: A Hispanic Women's Liberation Theology* (Minneapolis: Fortress, 1993), 63.

34. Terry Kershaw, "Afrocentrism and the Afrocentric Method," *Western Journal of Black Studies* 16, no. 3 (1992): 160–68.

35. West, *Wounds of the Spirit*, 7. Zora Neale Hurston in her discussion of research in her autobiography, *Dust Tracks on a Road*, relayed her difficulty in soliciting information about black southern folk culture when she approached community members in southern Florida using language and communication strategies that ran counter to the values of the community.

36. Paulo Freire, *Pedagogy of the Oppressed*, rev. ed., trans. and ed. M. B. Ramos (New York: Continuum, 1970, 1997), 24.

37. Emilie Townes, "Womanist Theology: Dancing with Twisted Hip," in *Introduction to Christian Theology: Contemporary North American Perspectives*, ed. Roger A. Badham (Louisville: Westminster John Knox Press: 1998), 213.

38. Jim Thomas, *Doing Critical Ethnography* (Newbury Park, CA: Sage Publications, 1993), 2–3.

39. Riggs, *Awake, Arise, and Act*, 77.

40. Freire, *Pedagogy of the Oppressed*, 12–13.

41. Ibid., 186.

42. For an in-depth account of transformative teaching-learning contexts and pedagogies, see bell hooks, *Teaching to Transgress: Education as the Practice of Freedom* (New York: Routledge, 1994), and Katherine Allen, Stacey Floyd-Thomas, and Laura Gillman, "Teaching to Transform: From Volatility to Solidarity in an Interdisciplinary Family Studies Classroom," *Family Relations* 50, no. 4 (2001): 324–25.

43. Collins, *Black Feminist Thought*, 263.

44. For a fuller description of the pedagogical implications of Cannon's Social Strata Inventory, see Allen, Floyd-Thomas, and Gillman, "Teaching to Transform," 317–25.

45. For a fuller description of this dialectical phenomenon, see Peter Berger, *The Sacred Canopy* (New York: Anchor Books, 1969).

Chapter 3: Black Women's Historiography

1. Karen Baker-Fletcher, "Dusting Off the Texts: Historical Resources for Womanist Ethics," *Annual of the Society of Christian Ethics* 14 (1994): 291.

2. Katie G. Cannon, *Katie's Canon: Womanism and the Soul of the Black Community* (New York: Continuum, 1995), 125.

3. For a critical analysis of this phenomenon, see Anthony B. Pinn, *African American Humanist Principles: Living and Thinking Like the Children of Nimrod* (New York: Palgrave, 2004).

4. Jacqueline D. Carr-Hamilton. "Notes on the Black Womanist Dilemma," *Journal of Religious Thought* 45, no. 1 (1998): 67. For further treatment of this observation, see Deborah Gray White's *Ar'n't I a Woman: Female Slaves in the Plantation South* (New York: Norton, 1985); Darlene Clark Hine and Kathleen Thompson's *A Shining Thread of Hope: The History of Black Women in America* (New York: Broadway Books, 1999); Evelyn Brooks Higginbotham's "African American Women's History and Metalanguage of Race," *Signs* 17, no. 21 (1992): 251–74, and "Beyond the Sound of Silence: Afro-American Women in History," *Gender and History* 1, no. 1 (Spring 1989): 131–39

5. G. W. F. Hegel, *The Philosophy of History* (New York: Dover, 1956), 93, 99.

6. David Hume, *The Philosophical Works*, edited by T. H. Green and T. H. Grose, vol. 3 (Aalen: Scientia Verlag, 1964), 252.

7. Immanuel Chukwudi Eze, ed., *Race and the Enlightenment* (Cambridge, MA: Blackwell, 1997), 38–78.

8. John Morely, *The Works of Voltaire: A Contemporary Version,* notes by Tobias Smollett, trans. William F. Fleming, vol. 19, part 2 (New York: Dingwall-Roch, 1927), 240–41.

9. Thomas Jefferson, *Notes on the State of Virginia,* ed. William Peden (Chapel Hill: University of North Carolina Press, 1954), 138–39.

10. Roy P. Basler, ed., *The Collected Works of Abraham Lincoln,* vol. 3 (New Brunswick, NJ: Rutgers University Press, 1953), 145–46.

11. Andrew Greeley, *The Irish Americans: The Rise to Money and Power* (New York: Harper and Row, 1981), 88.

12. Benjamin Munn Ziegler, *Desegregation and the Supreme Court* (Boston: D. C. Heath, 1958), 37.

13. "White Supremacists Who Once Occupied the White House," *Journal of Blacks in Higher Education* 24 (Summer 1999): 76–77.

14. Some key examples of general histories of African Americans that are representative of the "Negro History" school of historiography from the nineteenth and twentieth century are: James W. C. Pennington, *Text Book of the Origin and History of the Colored People* (Detroit: Negro History Press, 1841); William T. Alexander, *History of the Colored Race in America* (New York: Negro Universities Press, 1887, 1968); Harold M. Tarver, *The Negro in the History of the United States from the Beginnings of the English Settlements in 1607, to the Present Time* (Austin, TX: The State Print Co., 1905); E. A. Johnson, *School History of the Negro Race* (Philadelphia: Sherman and Co., 1893); George W. Williams, *History of the Negro Race in America*, 2 vols. (New York: Arno Press, 1882; reprinted 1968); Booker T. Washington, *The Story of the Negro: The Rise of the Race from Slavery*, 2 vols. (New York: 1909); Willis D. Weatherford, *The Negro from Africa to America* (New York, 1924); Benjamin Brawley, *A Short History of the American Negro* (New York, 1913); Merle R. Eppse, *The Negro, Too, in American History* (Chicago, 1939); Edwin R. Embree, *Brown Americans: The Story of a Tenth of the Nation* (New York, 1945); and J. A. Rogers, *World's Great Men of Color*, 2 vols. (New York, 1946; reprinted 1996).

15. The most representative general works of black history which hold both historiographical and information value are: Carter G. Woodson, *The Negro in Our History*, 10th ed. (1922: reprinted, Washington, DC, 1962); W. E. B. Du Bois, *Black Folk, Then and Now: An Essay in the History and Sociology of the Negro Race* (New York, 1939); Roi Ottley, *Black Odyssey* (New York, 1948); Rayford Logan, *The Negro in the United States* (New York, 1957); Lerone Bennett, *Before the Mayflower*, rev. ed. (1962; reprinted Chicago, 1987); J. Saunders Redding, *They Came in Chains*, rev. ed. (New York, 1952; 1973); William Z. Foster, *The Negro People in American History* (New York, 1970); Benjamin Quarles, *The Negro in the Making of America* (New York, 1964); August Meier and Elliot Rudwick, *From Plantation to Ghetto: An Interpretive History of American Negroes*, 3rd ed. (New York, 1976); Nathan I. Huggins, *Black Odyssey: The Afro-Americans' Ordeal in Slavery* (New York, 1977); Phillip S. Foner, *History of Black Americans*, 3 vols. (Westport, CT, 1975); Vincent Harding, *There Is a River: The Black Struggle for Freedom in America* (New York, 1981); Mary Frances Berry and John Blassingame, *Long Memory: The Black Experience in America* (New York, 1982); and John Hope Franklin and Alfred A. Moss Jr., *From Slavery to Freedom: A History of African Americans*, 8th ed. (1947; Boston, 2000).

16. Vincent Harding, *Beyond Chaos: Black History and the Search for a New Land*, in *Major Problems in African-American History*, ed. Thomas C. Holt and Elsa Barkley Brown (Boston: Houghton Mifflin, 2000), 1:8.

17. Ibid., 9.

18. In womanist metaethics, the answering of the "So what?" question is the lynchpin for satisfying the why-crisis of any moral problem. The answer to this question must take into account the *pathos* (feelings), *logos* (reason), *ethos* (values), and *theos* (ultimate concern) of an otherwise apathetic audience who must be logically persuaded and morally compelled to use their agency to address and resolve a moral problem in which they have been complicit.

19. Katie G. Cannon, *The Womanist Theology Primer — Remembering What We Never Knew: The Epistemology of Womanist Theology* (Louisville: Women's Ministries Program Area, National Ministries Division, Presbyterian Church [U.S.A.], 2001), 17.

20. Ibid.

21. Yvonne Chireau, "Hidden Traditions: Black Religion, Magic, and Alternative Spiritual Beliefs in Womanist Perspective," *Journal of the Interdenominational Theological Center* (Spring 1995): 67.

22. For a representation of the classic historical works on American slavery, see Herbert Aptheker, *American Negro Slave Revolts* (New York: International Publishers, 1969); Eugene D. Genovese, *Roll, Jordan, Roll: The World the Slaves Made* (New York: Pantheon Books, 1974); John W. Blassingame, *The Slave Community: Plantation Life in the Antebellum South* (New York: Oxford University Press, 1979).

23. For a further discussion about the struggle over issues of power, equality, and freedom between the North and South during the antebellum and Civil War eras, see W. E. B. Du Bois, *Black Reconstruction: An Essay Toward a History of the Part Which Black Folk Played in the Attempt to Reconstruct Democracy in America, 1860–1880* (New York: S. A. Russell, 1956, 1935); Eric Foner, *Free Soil, Free Labor, Free Men: The Ideology of the Republican Party before the Civil War* (London: Oxford University Press, 1971); James M. McPherson, *Battle Cry of Freedom: The Civil War Era* (New York: Oxford University Press, 1988); George M. Fredrickson, *The Inner Civil War: Northern Intellectuals and the Crisis of the Union* (1965; repr., Urbana: University of Illinois Press, 1993); and John Hope Franklin, *The Militant South: 1800–1861*, rev. ed. (1956; repr., Urbana: University of Illinois, 2002).

24. V. P. Franklin, *Living Our Stories, Telling Our Truths* (New York: Scribner, 1995), 11–12.

25. Joan M. Martin, *More Than Chains and Toil: A Christian Work Ethic of Enslaved Women* (Louisville: Westminster John Knox, 2000), 11.

26. bell hooks, *Outlaw Culture: Resisting Representations* (New York: Routledge, 1994), 4–5.

27. Martin, *More Than Chains and Toil*, 11.

28. Twelve percent of all existing slave narratives were written or dictated by black women, according to Yuval Taylor, ed., *I Was Born a Slave:*

An Anthology of Classic Slave Narratives, 1770–1849 (Chicago: Lawrence Hill Books, 1999), xvi.

29. James Cone, *God of the Oppressed*, rev. ed. (1975; Maryknoll, NY: Orbis Books, 1997), 52.

30. For the extended outline of Olney's anatomy of a slave narrative, see James Olney, "'I Was Born': Slave Narratives, Their Status as Autobiography and as Literature," in *The Slave's Narrative*, ed. Charles T. Davis and Henry Louis Gates Jr. (New York: Oxford University Press, 1985), 152–53.

31. Notable exceptions include liberation theologian Dwight N. Hopkins, *Down, Up, and Over: Slave Religion and Black Theology* (Minneapolis: Fortress, 2000), and Christian ethicist Riggins R. Earl Jr., *Dark Symbols, Obscure Signs: God, Self, and Community in the Slave Mind* (Maryknoll, NY: Orbis Books, 1993).

32. The term "neo-slave narrative" originated in the work of John Edgar Wideman. According to Wideman, the classic slave narratives of the eighteenth and nineteenth centuries had a progeny of countless texts that modeled the form and frame of the early slave narrative as it depicted the encounter of black life with political struggle. These best-sellers, while encapsulating the design and climax of the slave narratives, also were appealing to white audiences though read in large part by black audiences as well.

33. For a comprehensive consideration of his narrative method, see Scott C. Williamson, *The Narrative Life: The Moral and Religious Thought of Frederick Douglass* (Macon, GA: Mercer University Press, 2002).

34. White, *Ar'n't I a Woman?* 8.

35. Stephanie M. H. Camp, *Closer to Freedom: Enslaved Women and Everyday Resistance in the Plantation South* (Chapel Hill: University of North Carolina Press, 2004), 3.

36. Ibid., 7.

37. According Cornel West, "Constantinian Christianity" is the institutionalized collusion between church and state, wherein the legal power of the state and the legitimizing power of Christian rhetoric have persecuted marginalized peoples (particularly Jews and blacks) while privileging a select elite. For a thoroughgoing analysis of this concept, see Cornel West, *Democracy Matters: Winning the Fight against Imperialism* (New York: Penguin, 2004), 148.

38. Public Broadcasting Services Online, "Africans in America, Part 4 — 1831–1865: Nell Irvin Painter on Soul Murder and Slavery," *www.pbs.org/wgbh/aia/part4/4i3084.html.*

39. Ibid.

40. Painter credits psychiatrist Leonard Shengold for the term "soul murder." For a complete exploration of this psychiatric phenomenon, see Leonard

Shengold, *Soul Murder: The Effects of Child Abuse and Deprivation* (New York: Fawcett Columbine, 1989).

41. Harriet Jacobs [Linda Brent, pseud.], *Incidents in the Life of a Slave Girl,* 1st Signet Classic Printing (New York: Penguin, 2000), 92–93.

42. Ibid.

43. Melvin Dixon, "Singing Swords: The Literary Legacy of Slavery," in *The Slave's Narrative,* ed. Charles T. Davis and Henry Louis Gates Jr. (New York: Oxford University Press, 1985), 302.

44. Oliver Gilbert as quoted in Nell Irvin Painter, *Sojourner Truth: A Life, A Symbol* (New York: Norton, 1996), 29.

45. W. Noland Walker, "Episode I — There Is a River," *This Far by Faith: African American Spiritual Journeys* (San Francisco: California Newsreel, 2003).

46. Ibid.

47. Ibid.

48. Olney, " 'I Was Born,' " 153.

49. Emilie M. Townes, *Womanist Justice, Womanist Hope* (Atlanta: Scholars Press, 1993), 30.

50. Ibid., 30–31.

51. Ibid., 31.

52. Jacobs [Linda Brent, pseud.], *Incidents in the Life of a Slave Girl,* 91.

53. Ibid., 112.

54. Ibid., 142.

55. Ibid., 166.

56. Ibid., 158.

57. Ibid., 168.

58. Ibid., 171,

59. Yuval Taylor, introduction to *I Was Born a Slave: An Anthology of Classic Slave Narratives,* vol. 2, ed. Yuval Taylor (Edinburgh, Scotland: Payback Press, 1999), xviii.

60. Walker, "Episode I — There Is a River."

61. Painter, *Soujourner Truth,* 75.

62. Ibid. Painter also highlights that in the development of black historiography the voices of black women, particularly those who were preachers, were obscured. Since the motivation of much of black historiography was to chart the deleterious effects of racial injustice and few black female preachers of the time (like Jarena Lee and Julia Foote) addressed issues of race as their primary concerns, their voices are erased from history. But it is only through narratives like Sojourner Truth's that we might see evidence of the way in which these women erected pulpits with their presence and audacity to speak truth to power wherever they were.

63. Jacobs, *Incidents in the Life of a Slave Girl,* 227.

64. Rosetta Ross, *Witnessing and Testifying: Black Women, Religion, and Civil Rights* (Minneapolis: Fortress, 2002), 13.

65. Ibid., 14.

66. Townes, *Womanist Justice, Womanist Hope*, 20.

67. Henry Louis Gates Jr., "Introduction: On Bearing Witness," in *Bearing Witness: Selections from African-American Autobiography in the Twentieth Century*, ed. Henry Louis Gates Jr. (New York: Pantheon, 1991), 3.

68. Ibid., 4.

69. Robert Michael Franklin, *Liberating Visions: Human Fulfillment and Social Justice in African-American Thought* (Minneapolis: Fortress Press, 1989), 2.

70. Ibid., 3.

71. Townes, *Womanist Justice, Womanist Hope*, 18–19.

72. Ibid., 20.

73. Ibid., 23.

74. Ross, *Witnessing and Testifying*, 223, 224.

75. Hazel V. Carby, *Cultures in Babylon: Black Britain and African America* (London: Verso, 1999), 67–68.

76. "Web of mutuality" is a concept of the late Rev. Dr. Martin Luther King Jr., who professed that the beloved community was a world wherein every human being transcendently connected to one another. See Martin Luther King, "A Christmas Sermon on Peace" (1967), as quoted in *A Testament of Hope: The Essential Writings of Martin Luther King Jr.*, ed. James M. Washington (New York: HarperCollins, 1986).

77. Robin D. G. Kelley, *Race Rebels: Culture, Politics, and the Black Working Class* (New York: Free Press, 1994), 55–76.

78. Rosa Parks, with Gregory J. Reed, *Quiet Strength: The Faith, the Hope, and the Heart of a Woman Who Changed a Nation* (Grand Rapids, MI: Zondervan, 1994), 32.

79. Ibid., 31.

80. Ibid., 70.

81. Douglas Brinkley, *Rosa Parks* (New York: Viking, 2000), 68.

82. Ibid.

83. Ibid., 16–20.

84. Ibid., 193.

85. Ibid.

86. Barbara Ransby, *Ella Baker and the Black Freedom Movement: A Radical Democratic Vision* (Chapel Hill: University of North Carolina, 2003), 241–42.

87. Ibid., 245.

88. Ibid., 241–46.

89. Ibid., 112.

90. Ibid., 292.

91. Ibid., 295.

92. Emancipatory historiography finds its roots in the interdisciplinary scholarship of feminist and womanist ethicists such as Beverly Wildung Harrison, Katie G. Cannon, and Marcia Riggs.

93. Katie G. Cannon, "Emancipatory Historiography," in *The Dictionary of Feminist Theologies,* ed. Letty M. Russell and J. Shannon Clarkson (Louisville: Westminster John Knox, 1996), 81.

94. bell hooks, *Sisters of the Yam* (Boston: South End, 1993), 3.

95. Ibid., 2.

96. Toni Morrison, ed., *Race-ing Justice, En-gendering Power* (New York: Pantheon, 1992), xvi.

97. Ibid.

98. E. Frances White, *Dark Continent of Our Bodies: Black Feminism and the Politics of Respectability* (Philadelphia: Temple University Press, 2001), 15.

99. James Baldwin, "White Man's Guilt," in *James Baldwin: Collected Essays,* ed. Toni Morrison (New York: Library of America, 1998), 723.

100. hooks, *Sisters of the Yam,* 5.

101. Toni Cade Bambara, *The Black Woman: An Anthology* (New York: Penguin, 1970), 109.

102. Daphne C. Wiggins, *Righteous Content: Black Women Speak of Church and Faith* (New York: New York University Press, 2004), 175.

103. Deborah Gray White, *Too Heavy a Load: Black Women in Defense of Themselves, 1894–1994* (New York: Norton, 1999), 15.

Selected Bibliography

Books

Andersen, Margaret. *Thinking about Women: Sociological Perspectives on Sex and Gender.* Boston: Allyn and Bacon, 1983, 2002.

Anderson, Victor. *Beyond Ontological Blackness: An Essay on African American Religious and Cultural Criticism.* New York: Continuum, 1995.

Anzaldúa, Gloria, ed. *Making Face, Making Soul.* San Francisco: Aunt Lute Foundation, 1990.

Aptheker, Herbert. *American Negro Slave Revolts.* New York: International Publishers, 1969.

Asante, Molefi Kete. *The Afrocentric Idea.* Philadelphia: Temple University Press, 1998.

Badham, Roger A., ed. *Introduction to Christian Theology: Contemporary North American Perspectives.* Louisville: Westminster John Knox, 1998.

Bambara, Toni Cade. *The Black Woman: An Anthology.* New York: Penguin, 1970.

Basler, Roy P., ed. *The Collected Works of Abraham Lincoln,* vol. 3. New Brunswick, NJ: Rutgers University Press, 1953.

Berger, Peter. *The Sacred Canopy.* New York: Anchor Books, 1969.

Blassingame, John W. *The Slave Community: Plantation Life in the Antebellum South.* New York: Oxford University Press, 1979.

Brinkley, Douglas. *Rosa Parks.* New York: Viking, 2000.

Camp, Stephanie M. H. *Closer to Freedom: Enslaved Women and Everyday Resistance in the Plantation South.* Chapel Hill: University of North Carolina Press, 2004.

Cannon, Katie G. *Black Womanist Ethics.* Atlanta: Scholars Press, 1988.

———. *Katie's Canon: Womanism and the Soul of the Black Community.* New York: Continuum, 1995.

———. *Teaching Preaching: Isaac Rufus Clark and Black Sacred Rhetoric.* New York: Continuum, 2002.

————. *The Womanist Theology Primer — Remembering What We Never Knew: The Epistemology of Womanist Theology.* Louisville: Women's Ministries Program Area, National Ministries Division, Presbyterian Church (U.S.A.), 2001.

Carby, Hazel V. *Cultures in Babylon: Black Britain and African America.* London: Verso, 1999.

Christian, Barbara. *Black Feminist Criticism: Perspectives on Black Women Writers.* New York: Pergamon Press, 1985.

Collins, Patricia Hill. *Black Feminist Thought: Knowledge, Consciousness, and the Politics of Empowerment.* Boston: Unwin Hyman, 1990.

Comstock, Gary David. *A Whosoever Church: Welcoming Lesbians and Gay Men into African American Congregations.* Louisville: Westminster John Knox, 2001.

Cone, James. *God of the Oppressed,* rev. ed. Maryknoll, NY: Orbis Books, 1997.

————, and Gayraud Wilmore, eds. *Black Theology: A Documentary History.* 2 vols. Maryknoll, NY: Orbis Books, 1993.

Davies, Carole Boyce. *Black Women, Writing and Identity: Migrations of the Subject.* New York: Routledge, 1994.

Davis, Charles T., and Henry Louis Gates Jr., eds. *The Slave's Narrative.* New York: Oxford University Press, 1985.

Du Bois, W. E. B. *The Souls of Black Folk.* New York: Vintage, 1903, 1982.

————. *Black Reconstruction: An Essay Toward a History of the Part Which Black Folk Played in the Attempt to Reconstruct Democracy in America, 1860–1880.* New York: S. A. Russell, 1956.

Earl, Riggins R., Jr. *Dark Symbols, Obscure Signs: God, Self, and Community in the Slave Mind.* Maryknoll, NY: Orbis Books, 1993.

Eze, Immanuel Chukwudi, ed. *Race and the Enlightenment.* Cambridge, MA: Blackwell, 1997.

Felder, Cain Hope, ed. *Stony the Way We Trod: African American Biblical Interpretation.* Minneapolis: Fortress, 1991.

Fowler, James W. *Stages of Faith: The Psychology of Human Development and the Quest for Meaning.* New York: Harper & Row, 1981.

Foner, Eric. *Free Soil, Free Labor, Free Men: The Ideology of the Republican Party before the Civil War.* London: Oxford University Press, 1971.

Franklin, Robert Michael. *Liberating Visions: Human Fulfillment and Social Justice in African-American Thought.* Minneapolis: Fortress Press, 1989.

Franklin, V. P. *Living Our Stories, Telling Our Truths.* New York: Scribner, 1995.

Freire, Paulo. *Pedagogy of the Oppressed.* Trans. and ed. by M. B. Ramos. New York: Continuum, 1970, 1997.

Gates, Henry Louis, Jr., ed. *Bearing Witness: Selections from African-American Autobiography in the Twentieth Century.* New York: Pantheon, 1991.

Genovese, Eugene D. *Roll, Jordan, Roll: The World the Slaves Made.* New York: Pantheon Books, 1974.

Gilkes, Cheryl Townsend. *"If It Wasn't for the Women...": Black Women's Experience and Womanist Culture in Church and Community.* Maryknoll, NY: Orbis Books, 2001.

Gould, Stephen Jay. *The Mismeasure of Man.* New York: W. W. Norton & Company, 1981.

Greeley, Andrew. *The Irish Americans: The Rise to Money and Power.* New York: Harper and Row, 1981.

Harrison, Beverly Wildung. *Making the Connections: Essays in Feminist Social Ethics.* Ed. Carol S. Robb. Boston: Beacon Press, 1985.

Hegel, G. W. F. *The Philosophy of History.* New York: Dover, 1956.

Henke, Suzette A. *Shattered Subjects: Trauma and Testimony in Women's Life-Writing.* New York: St. Martin's Press, 1998.

Holmes, Barbara. *A Private Woman in Public Spaces: Barbara Jordan's Speeches on Ethics, Public Religion, and Law.* Harrisburg, PA: Trinity Press, 2000.

hooks, bell. *Feminist Theory: From Margin to Center.* Boston: South End, 1984.

———. *Outlaw Culture: Resisting Representations.* New York: Routledge, 1994.

———. *Sisters of the Yam.* Boston: South End, 1993.

———. *Teaching to Transgress: Education as the Practice of Freedom.* New York: Routledge, 1994.

———. *Yearning: Race, Gender, and Cultural Politics.* Boston: South End Press, 1990.

Hopkins, Dwight N. *Down, Up, and Over: Slave Religion and Black Theology.* Minneapolis: Fortress, 2000.

Hull, Gloria, Pat Bell Scott, and Barbara Smith. *All the Women Are White, All the Blacks Are Men, But Some of Us Are Brave.* Old Westbury, NY: Feminist Press, 1982.

Hume, David. *The Philosophical Works.* Ed. T. H. Green and T. H. Grose, vol. 3. Aalen: Scientia Verlag, 1964.

Hurston, Zora Neale. *Mules and Men.* New York: HarperCollins, 1990.

———. *Their Eyes Were Watching God.* New York: Harper and Row, 1937, 1990.

Isasi-Díaz, Ada María. *En la Lucha — In the Struggle: A Hispanic Women's Liberation Theology.* Minneapolis: Fortress Press, 1993.

Jacobs, Harriet [Linda Brent, pseud.], *Incidents in the Life of a Slave Girl.* New York: Penguin, 2000.

Jefferson, Thomas. *Notes on the State of Virginia.* Ed. William Peden. Chapel Hill: University of North Carolina Press, 1954.

Keating, AnaLouise. *Women Reading Women Writing: Self-Invention in Paula Gunn Allen, Gloria Anzaldúa and Audre Lorde.* Philadelphia: Temple University Press, 1996.

Kelley, Robin D. G. *Race Rebels: Culture, Politics, and the Black Working Class.* New York: Free Press, 1994.

Kirk-Duggan, Cheryl A. *Exorcising Evil: A Womanist Perspective on the Spirituals.* Maryknoll, NY: Orbis Books, 1997.

Ladner, Joyce A., ed. *The Death of White Sociology.* New York: Random House, 1973.

Lawrence-Lightfoot, Sara. *I've Known Rivers: Lives of Loss and Liberation.* Reading, MA: Addison Wesley, 1994.

Martin, Joan M. *More Than Chains and Toil: A Christian Work Ethic of Enslaved Women.* Louisville: Westminster John Knox, 2000.

Morely, John. *The Works of Voltaire: A Contemporary Version.* Notes by Tobias Smollett. Translated by William F. Fleming, vol. 19, part 2. New York: Dingwall-Roch, 1927.

Morrison, Toni, ed. *Race-ing Justice, En-gendering Power.* New York: Pantheon, 1992.

———. *James Baldwin: Collected Essays.* New York: Library of America, 1998.

Olney, James. " 'I Was Born': Slave Narratives, Their Status as Autobiography and as Literature." In *The Slave's Narrative,* ed. Charles T. Davis and Henry Louis Gates Jr., 152–53. New York: Oxford University Press, 1985.

Painter, Nell Irvin. *Sojourner Truth: A Life, a Symbol.* New York: Norton, 1996.

Parks, Rosa, with Gregory J. Reed. *Quiet Strength: The Faith, the Hope, and the Heart of a Woman Who Changed a Nation.* Grand Rapids: Zondervan, 1994.

Pinn, Anthony B. *African American Humanist Principles: Living and Thinking Like the Children of Nimrod.* New York: Palgrave, 2004.

Radford-Hill, Sheila. *Further to Fly: Black Women and the Politics of Empowerment.* Minneapolis: University of Minnesota Press, 2000.

Ransby, Barbara. *Ella Baker and the Black Freedom Movement: A Radical Democratic Vision.* Chapel Hill: University of North Carolina, 2003.

Riggs, Marcia Y. *Awake, Arise, and Act: A Womanist Call for Black Liberation.* Cleveland: Pilgrim, 1994.

———. *Plenty Good Room: Women Versus Male Power in the Black Church.* Cleveland: Pilgrim, 2003.

Ross, Rosetta. *Witnessing and Testifying: Black Women, Religion, and Civil Rights.* Minneapolis: Fortress Press, 2002.

Russell, Letty M., ed. *Feminist Interpretation of the Bible.* Louisville: Westminster, 1985.

———, and J. Shannon Clarkson, eds. *The Dictionary of Feminist Theologies.* Louisville: Westminster John Knox Press, 1996.

Sanders, Cheryl, ed. *Living the Intersection: Womanism and Afrocentrism in Theology.* Minneapolis: Fortress Press, 1995.

Shengold, Leonard. *Soul Murder: The Effects of Child Abuse and Deprivation.* New York: Fawcett Columbine, 1989.

Spretnak, Charlene. *The Politics of Women's Spirituality.* New York: Anchor Press, 1982.

Stivers, Robert, Christine Gudorf, Alice Evans, and Robert Evans, eds. *Christian Ethics: A Case Method Approach,* 2nd ed. Maryknoll, NY: Orbis Books, 1994.

Taylor, Yuval, ed. *I Was Born a Slave: An Anthology of Classic Slave Narratives, 1770–1849.* Chicago: Lawrence Hill Books, 1999.

Thomas, Jim. *Doing Critical Ethnography.* Newbury Park, CA: Sage Publications, 1993.

Townes, Emilie. *Womanist Justice, Womanist Hope.* Atlanta: Scholars Press, 1993.

Townes, Emilie, ed. *A Troubling in My Soul: Womanist Perspectives on Evil and Suffering.* Maryknoll, NY: Orbis Books, 1993.

———. *Embracing the Spirit: Womanist Perspectives on Hope, Salvation, and Transformation.* Maryknoll, NY: Orbis Books, 1997.

Walker, Alice. *In Search of Our Mothers' Gardens: Womanist Prose.* San Diego: Harcourt Brace Jovanovich, 1983.

———. *The Color Purple.* New York: Washington Square, 1982.

Washington, Harold C., Susan Lochrie Graham, and Pamela Thimmes, eds. *Escaping Eden: New Feminist Perspectives on the Bible.* New York: New York University Press, 1999.

Washington, James M., ed. *A Testament of Hope: The Essential Writings of Martin Luther King Jr.* New York: HarperCollins, 1986.

Weems, Renita J. *Battered Love: Marriage, Sex, and Violence in the Hebrew Prophets.* Minneapolis: Fortress, 1995.

———. *I Asked for Intimacy: Stories of Blessings, Betrayals, and Birthings.* San Diego: LuraMedia, 1993.

West, Cornel. *Race Matters.* Boston: Beacon, 1993.

———. *Democracy Matters: Winning the Fight against Imperialism.* New York: Penguin, 2004.

West, Traci C. *Wounds of the Spirit: Black Women, Violence and Resistance Ethics.* New York: New York University Press, 1999.

White, Deborah Gray. *Ar'n't I a Woman? Female Slaves in the Plantation South.* Rev. ed. New York: Norton, 1999.

———. *Too Heavy a Load: Black Women in Defense of Themselves, 1894–1994.* New York: Norton, 1999.

White, E. Frances. *Dark Continent of Our Bodies: Black Feminism and the Politics of Respectability.* Philadelphia: Temple University Press, 2001.

Wiggins, Daphne C. _Righteous Content: Black Women Speak of Church and Faith._ New York: New York University Press, 2004.

Williams, Delores. _Sisters in the Wilderness: The Challenge of Womanist God-Talk._ Maryknoll, NY: Orbis Books, 1993.

Williamson, Scott C. _The Narrative Life: The Moral and Religious Thought of Frederick Douglass._ Macon, GA: Mercer University Press, 2002.

Zack, Naomi. _Race and Mixed Race._ Philadelphia: Temple University Press, 1993.

Ziegler, Benjamin Munn. _Desegregation and the Supreme Court._ Boston: D. C. Heath, 1958.

Articles

Allen, Katherine, Stacey Floyd-Thomas, and Laura Gillman, "Teaching to Transform: From Volatility to Solidarity in an Interdisciplinary Family Studies Classroom." _Family Relations_ 50, no. 4 (2001): 317–25.

Alliaume, Karen Timble. "The Risks of Repeating Ourselves: Reading Feminist/Womanist Figures of Jesus." _Cross Currents_ 48, no. 2 (Summer 1998): 198–217.

Austin, Deborah A. "In the Middle of Everyday Life: The Spaces Black Clergywomen Create." _Journal of the Interdenominational Theological Center_ 22, no. 2 (Spring 1995): 209–29.

Baker, Dori Grinenko. "Girlfriend Theology: God-Talk across Religious Borders." _Religious Education_ 95, no. 3 (Summer 2000): 320–39.

Baker-Fletcher, Garth. "Xodus Musings: Reflections on Womanist Tar Baby Theology." _Theology Today_ 50, no. 1 (1993): 38–44.

Baker-Fletcher, Karen. "Dusting Off the Texts: Historical Resources for Womanist Ethics." _Annual of the Society of Christian Ethics_ 14 (1994): 291–98.

———. "Rooted in the Land." _The Other Side_ 31, no. 5 (September–October 1995): 17–21.

———. "Tar Baby and Womanist Theology." _Theology Today_ 50, no. 1 (April 1993): 29–37.

———. "The Difference Race Makes." _Journal of Feminist Studies in Religion_ 8, no. 2 (1992): 7–15.

———. "Womanism, Afro-centrism, and the Reconstruction of Black Womanhood." _Journal of the Interdenominational Theological Center_ 22, no. 2 (Spring 1995): 183–97.

Becker, William H. "Celie as Spiritual Wrestler." _Journal of the Interdenominational Theological Center_ 22, no. 2 (Spring 1995): 147–81.

Berger, Teresa. "Ecumenism: Postconfessional? Consciously Contextual?" *Theology Today* 53, no. 2 (1996): 213–19.

Brooks, Evelyn. "Religion, Politics, and Gender: The Leadership of Nannie Helen Burroughs." *Journal of Religious Thought* 44, no. 2 (1998): 7–22.

Brown, Kelly Delaine. "God Is as Christ Does: Toward a Womanist Theology." *Journal of Religious Thought* 46, no. 1 (Summer–Fall 1989): 7–16.

Browne, Joy Elizabeth. "Theology and Literary Criticism in the Womanist Mode." *Journal of the Interdenominational Theological Center* 22, no. 2 (Spring 1995): 115–28.

Burrow, Rufus, Jr. "Development of Womanist Theology: Some Chief Characteristics." *Asbury Theological Journal* 54, no. 1 (Spring 1999): 41–57.

———. "Toward Womanist Theology and Ethics." *Journal of Feminist Studies in Religion* 15, no. 1 (1999): 77–95.

———. "Womanist Theology and Ethics." *Encounter* 59, nos. 1–2 (1998): 157–75.

Cannon, Katie G., et al. "Metalogues and Dialogues: Teaching the Womanist Idea." *Journal of Feminist Studies in Religion* 8, no. 2 (1992): 125–51.

Carpenter, Delores C. "Black Women in Religious Institutions: A Historical Summary from Slavery to the 1960s." *Journal of Religious Thought* 46, no. 2 (Winter–Summer 1989–90): 7–27.

Carr-Hamilton, Jacqueline D. "Notes on the Black Womanist Dilemma." *Journal of Religious Thought* 45, no. 1 (1988): 67–69.

Chireau, Yvonne. "Hidden Traditions: Black Religion, Magic, and Alternative Spiritual Beliefs in Womanist Perspective." *Journal of the Interdenominational Theological Center* (Spring 1995): 65–88.

Clendenen, Avis, and Phillis Sheppard. "The Grace of Difference: A Dialogue between Sisters." *Chicago Theological Seminary Register* 89, no. 2 (Spring 1999): 1–12.

Coleman, Will. "Tribal Talk: Black Theology in Postmodern Configurations." *Theology Today* 50, no. 1 (1993): 68–77.

Crawford, A. Elaine. "Womanist Christology: Where Have We Come from and Where Are We Going?" *Review and Expositor* 95, no. 3 (1998): 367–82.

Dewey, Joanna, et al. "Respondents" [to Clarice J. Martin]. *Journal of Feminist Studies in Religion* 6, no. 2 (1990): 63–85.

Doak, Mary C. "Cornel West's Challenge to the Catholic Evasion of Black Theology." *Theological Studies* 63 (2002): 87–106.

Douglas, Kelly Brown. "A Womanist Looks at the Future Direction of Theological Discourse." *Anglican Theological Review* 76, no. 2 (1994): 225–31.

———. "Is Christ a Black Woman?" *The Other Side* 30, no. 2 (1994): 8–11, 54.

————. "Marginalized People, Liberating Perspectives: A Womanist Approach to Biblical Interpretation." *Anglican Theological Review* 83, no. 1 (Winter 2001): 41–47.

Estes-Hicks, Onita. "Henriette Delille: Free Woman of Color, Candidate for Roman Catholic Sainthood, Early Womanist." *Journal of the Interdenominational Theological Center* 22, no. 2 (Spring 1995): 41–54.

Eugene, Toinette M. "If You Get There before I Do! A Womanist Ethical Response to Sexual Violence and Abuse." *Journal of the Interdenominational Theological Center* 22, no. 2 (Spring 1995): 91–113.

————. "In This Here Place, We Flesh." *Daughters of Sarah* 22, no. 1 (Winter 1996): 6–15.

————. "Moral Values and Black Womanists." *Journal of Religious Thought* 45, no. 4 (1988): 23–34.

————. "On 'Difference' and the Dream of Pluralist Feminism in 'Appropriation and Reciprocity in Womanist/Mujerista/Feminist Work.'" *Journal of Feminist Studies in Religion* 8 (1992): 91–122.

Floyd-Thomas, Stacey, and Laura Gillman. "Subverting Forced Identities, Violent Acts and the Narrativity of Race: A Diasporic Analysis of Black Women's Radical Subjectivity in Three Novel Acts." *Journal of Black Studies* 32, no. 5 (2002): 528–56.

Gilkes, Cheryl Townsend. "To Sit and Die or to Stand and Live." *Journal of Religious Thought* 47, no. 2 (Winter–Summer 1990–91): 56–63.

"Gloria Naylor and Toni Morrison, a Conversation." *Southern Review* 21, no. 3 (July 1985): 593.

Goldsmith, Peter. "A Woman's Place Is in the Church." *Journal of Religious Thought* 46, no. 2 (Winter–Summer 1989–90): 53–69.

Haney, LaVerne J. "Praying Through: The Spiritual Narrative of Mother E. J. Dabney." *Journal of the Interdenominational Theological Center* 22, no. 2 (Spring 1995): 231–40.

Harding, Vincent. "Beyond Chaos: Black History and the Search for a New Land." In *Major Problems in African-American History,* ed. Thomas C. Holt and Elsa Barkley Brown. Boston: Houghton Mifflin, 2000.

Hine, Darlene Clark, and Kathleen Thompson. *A Shining Thread of Hope: The History of Black Women in America.* New York: Broadway Books, 1999.

Hinga, Teresa M. "African Feminist Theologies, the Global Village, and the Imperative of Solidarity across Borders." *Journal of Feminist Studies in Religion* 18, no. 1 (2002): 79–86.

Hopkins, Dwight N., and Linda E. Thomas. "Black Theology U.S.A. Revisited." *Journal of Theology for Southern Africa* 100 (March 1998): 61–85.

Howell, Nancy R. "Ecofeminism: What One Needs to Know." *Zygon* 32, no. 2 (1997): 231–41.

Jacques, Michele. "Testimony as Embodiment: Telling the Truth and Shaming the Devil." *Journal of the Interdenominational Theological Center* 22, no. 2 (Spring 1995): 129–45.

Jones-Warsaw, Koala. "Toward a Womanist Hermeneutic: A Reading of Judges 19–21." *Journal of the Interdenominational Theological Center* 22, no. 1 (Fall 1994): 18–35.

Kershaw, Terry. "Afrocentrism and the Afrocentric Method." *Western Journal of Black Studies* 16, no. 3 (1992): 160–68.

Kirk-Duggan, Cheryl A. "Ebonics as an Ethically Sound Discourse: A Solution, Not a Problem." *Annual of the Society of Christian Ethics* 18 (1998): 139–60.

Lincoln, C. Eric. *Black Muslims in America.* Boston: Beacon Press, 1961.

Maluleke, Tinyiko Sam. "Half a Century of African Christian Theologies." *Journal of Theology for Southern Africa* 99 (November 1997): 4–23.

Martin, Clarice J. "Womanist Interpretations of the New Testament." *Journal of Feminist Studies in Religion* 6, no. 2 (1990): 41–61.

Martin, Joan M. "A Womanist Investigation of the Work Ethic of Antebellum Enslaved Women, 1830–1865." *Journal of the Interdenominational Theological Center* 22, no. 2 (Spring 1995): 5–23.

———. "The Notion of Difference for Emerging Womanist Ethics: The Writings of Audre Lorde and bell hooks." *Journal of Feminist Studies in Religion* 9, nos. 1–2 (Spring–Fall 1993): 39–51.

———. "Re-Imagining the Church as Spiritual Institution." *Church and Society* 84 (May–June 1994): 52–59.

Masenya, Madipoane J. "African Womanist Hermeneutics." *Journal of Feminist Studies in Religion* 11, no. 1 (1995): 149–55.

McCrary, Carolyn L. "The Wholeness of Women: An African Woman's Story." *Journal of the Interdenominational Theological Center* 25, no. 3 (Spring 1998): 258–94.

Medine, Carolyn. "Memory, Narrative, and Peacemaking in Toni Morrison's Fiction." Paper presentation, Annual Meeting of the American Academy of Religion, Atlanta, November 23, 2003.

Morgan, Sue. "Race and the Appeal to Experience in Feminist Theology." *Modern Believing* 36, no. 2 (1995): 18–26.

Morrison, Toni. "Behind the Making of the Black Book." *Black World* 23 (February 1974): 86–90.

Oduyoye, Mercy Amba. "Re-Imagining the World: A Global Perspective." *Church and Society* 84 (May–June 1994): 82–93.

Orr, Deborah. "The Crone as Lover and Teacher: A Philosophical Reading of Zora Neale Hurston's *Their Eyes Were Watching God.*" *Journal of Feminist Studies in Religion* 18, no. 1 (2002): 25–50.

Paris, Peter J. "From Womanist Thought to Womanist Action." *Journal of Feminist Studies in Religion* 9, nos. 1–2 (1993): 115–25.

Pinn, Anthony B. "And Your Daughters Shall Prophesy: Public Speeches of Maria Stewart, 1832–1833." *Journal of the Interdenominational Theological Center* 22, no. 2 (Spring 1995): 55–64.

———. "Religion and 'America's Problem Child': Notes on Pauli Murray's Theological Development." *Journal of Feminist Studies in Religion* 15, no. 1 (1999): 21–39.

Riggs, Marcia. "Answering God's Call to Academe." *Journal of the Interdenominational Theological Center* 22, no. 2 (Spring 1995): 201–8.

Ronan, Marian. "Reclaiming Women's Experience: A Reading of Selected Christian Feminist Theologies." *Cross Currents* 48, no. 3 (Summer 1998): 218–29.

Russell-Robinson, Joyce. "Defiance and Hope: The Christian Temperament in Nineteenth-Century African-American Women's Narratives." *Journal of the Interdenominational Theological Center* 22, no. 2 (Spring 1995): 25–39.

Sanders, Cheryl J. "Womanist Ethics: Contemporary Trends and Themes." *Annual of the Society of Christian Ethics* 14 (1994): 299–305.

Sanders, Cheryl J., et al. "Roundtable Discussion: Christian Ethics and Theology in Womanist Perspective." *Journal of Feminist Studies in Religion* 5 (1989): 83–112.

Sawyer, Mary R. "Black Religion and Social Change: Women in Leadership Roles." *Journal of Religious Thought* 47, no. 2 (Winter–Summer 1990–91): 16–29.

Smith, Chandra Taylor. "Pragmatism and Womanist Theology: Interpretive Possibilities." *American Journal of Theology and Philosophy* 19, no. 2 (May 1998): 209–23.

Smith, Christine M. "Sin and Evil in Feminist Thought." *Theology Today* 50, no. 2 (1993): 208–19.

Smith, Pamela A. "Green Lap, Brown Embrace, Blue Body: The Ecospirituality of Alice Walker." *Cross Currents* 48, no. 4 (Winter 1998–99): 471–87.

Speller, Julia M. "Marginality within the Margins." *Chicago Theological Seminary Register* 89, no. 2 (Spring 1999): 13–24.

Stewart, Dianne M. "Rethinking Gospel and Culture." *Quarterly Review* 20, no. 2 (2000): 140–54.

Taylor, Yuval. Introduction to *I Was Born a Slave: An Anthology of Classic Slave Narratives, Vol. II,* ed. Yuval Taylor. Edinburgh, Scotland: Payback Press, 1999.

Thistlethwaite, Susan Brooks. "Virtual Reality Christianity." *Theology Today* 52, no. 2 (1995): 225–35.

Thomas, Linda E. "Womanist Theology, Epistemology, and a New Anthropological Paradigm." *Cross Currents* 48, no. 4 (Winter 1998–1999): 488–99.

Townes, Emilie M. "Searching for Paradise in a World of Theme Parks: Toward a Womanist Ethic of Care." *Lexington Theological Quarterly* 33, no. 3 (1998): 131–50.

Trulear, Harold Dean. "Reshaping Black Pastoral Theology: The Vision of Bishop Ida B. Robinson." *Journal of Religious Thought* 46, no. 1 (Summer–Fall 1989): 17–31.

Welch, Sharon D. "Biblical Interpretation in Christian Feminist Ethics." *Studia Theologica* 51, no. 1 (1997): 30–43.

Wells, April C. "The Church's Contribution to Patriarchy: Destruction of the Mental, Emotional, Spiritual, and Physical Health of Women." *Journal of the Interdenominational Theological Center* 25, no. 3 (Spring 1998): 110–38.

"White Supremacists Who Once Occupied the White House." *Journal of Blacks in Higher Education* 24 (Summer 1999): 76–77.

Williams, Carmen Braun, and Marsa Wiggins Frame. "Constructing New Realities: Integrating Womanist Traditions in Pastoral Counseling with African-American Women." *Pastoral Psychology* 47, no. 4 (1999): 303–14.

Williams, Delores S. "Womanist/Feminist Dialogue: Problems and Possibilities." *Journal of Feminist Studies in Religion* 9, nos. 1–2 (1993): 67–73.

Wimberly, Edward P. "Methods of Cross-Cultural Pastoral Care: Hospitality and Incarnation." *Journal of the Interdenominational Theological Center* 25, no. 3 (Spring 1998): 188–202.

Witherspoon, Kimmika Williams. "Carrying My Mother's Song." *The Other Side* 33, no. 2 (March–April 1997): 41–43.

Index